Why Don't
They Call Me?

JOB SEARCH WISDOM TO GET YOU UNSTUCK

MICHAEL PETRAS
http://www.job-interview-wisdom.com

ISBN: 1456544780
ISBN-13: 9781456544782
Library of Congress Control Number: 2011900787

Table of Contents

Introduction

You probably are holding this book in your hands because your job search has either hit a brick wall, or you are very dissatisfied with the way your job search is going.

You may have already read several worthy books about job hunting, or visited numerous websites. But no matter what you do...*nothing* seems to work.

Somehow, Murphy showed up at your door, plunked himself down in your favorite easy chair, grabbed the remote control, and just won't leave. For the next few days, I want you to set all that aside—*except for Murphy*.

It's time to get rid of him once and for all!

You are about to embark upon an enlightening course of action designed to lift your spirits, restore your hope, and maximize your chances of landing a job. In short, I'm going to share with you a step-by-step process that is the fastest way to find a job.

After all, you've endured this trial long enough...*right?*

If you are one of these 5 struggling job seekers this book will be a game-changer for you

1. People unemployed six months—*or longer*—who get very few job interviews.

2. People unemployed six months—*or longer*—who rarely, *if ever*, get a job offer.

3. People late in their career who suspect that age discrimination is the main reason they aren't being invited in for job interviews, let alone getting job offers.

4. People who have been fired or laid off who now struggle with guilt, depression, marital stress, low self-esteem, feelings of hopelessness, or simply lack motivation.

5. People who have lost their job after a long career with one company, and now find themselves out-of-step and out-of-date with the job search process.

Regardless of your job search dilemma, you undoubtedly are going through a very discouraging time. You may even be downright depressed about it.

What's worse, all areas of your life may seem out of balance and unfulfilling right now.

And that may be putting it mildly.

Looking for a job is a gut-wrenching, emotional experience. Our feelings can either motivate us to take massive action, or paralyze us into avoiding what we know **must** be done.

This book is a culmination of over twenty years of direct hiring experience as an executive recruiter and a regional sales director for a Fortune 500 company. It contains cutting edge ideas and actions steps that will work for you on both an intellectual *and* emotional level. You need equilibrium on both levels to enhance your job search prospects.

You'll get the most out of my job search strategy if you stick to the plan and follow my step by step process. Avoid skipping ahead or only reading those sections of greatest interest to you. Above all, do the action steps, even if they are uncomfortable for you. The idea is for you to get outside your comfort zones.

You may come to a section where you say to yourself, *"I already tried that and it didn't work for me."* Give it another chance, as I could share some critical information with you that will result in a completely different outcome.

Let me be your guide and walk beside you.

We're starting with a clean sheet of paper. Every detail of the job search process will be examined to make sure you're in the *right* place, at the *right* time, with your *best* game face on.

10 nagging problems that sabotage every job search

1. The fear, anxiety—*or shear panic*—of not knowing what more you can possibly do to find a job...especially after you've made a valiant effort to find one.

2. The inability to shrug off the pain of rejection and indifference.

3. Putting up with a lack of common courtesy from hiring authorities, gate keepers, past associates, and "friends".

4. Enduring unrealistic expectations of spouse, family members, and extended family.

5. Coping with the negative influence of the news media and other macro-trends.

6. Letting go of the past, embracing change, and developing optimism for the future.

7. Lacking time management discipline since no one is holding you accountable anymore.

8. Trouble breaking the chains of inaction and bad habits.

9. Worrying about things you have no control over.

10. Struggling with procrastination and risk avoidance.

Ever witness a great baseball player in a batting slump?

Batting slumps are extremely frustrating and humbling for a world-class athlete. Almost every ball player goes through a slump at some point during their career.

A player often tries to pull himself out of his slump by swinging the bat harder, going after inside pitches, changing his stance in the batter's box, choking up on the bat, or numerous other adjustments...usually to no avail.

The harder he tries to turn things around, the worst the batting slump gets. He keeps looking for *that one thing* that will make it all work for him again.

This is why professional baseball teams have batting coaches on their staff. Batting coaches observe the ball player in an analytical, unemotional way, and bring into equilibrium all the *little things* a batter must do to hit the ball—and most importantly—control where it goes.

My job hunting expertise will be of tremendous value to you at this sticking point in your career. As of this moment, I'm your batting coach. You simply need a fresh set of eyes to help you hit some singles and doubles.

I pledge to you my best work in helping you get your career back on track...*really fast.*

Ok...let's go...batter up!

Mike Petras
March 2011

Chapter 1:
How to Sooth the Pain of Losing Your Job

Jelly bread always falls jelly-side down.
~Murphy's Law

People who have never lost their job don't have a clue what it feels like. Unless you've lived through an extended period of unemployment, you simply can't relate.

For most folks, it's one of the greatest trials of their life.

Unfortunately, many people define themselves by what they do for a living. When you lose your job, your self-worth and self esteem are shaken to the core. The pain you suffer can be intense and similar to a death of a close friend or loved one.

In a way, part of you has died. As a result, you will likely experience…

The 8 stages of grief

1. Shock
2. Denial
3. Bargaining
4. Guilt
5. Anger
6. Depression
7. Resignation
8. Acceptance and Hope

How I survived the shock and embarrassment of getting fired

See if you can identify the eight stages of grief in my own job loss story. In 1995, I was fired from Damon Corporation as their national sales manager.

It happened on a Friday.

Shortly after lunch, the VP of Sales walked into my office, quietly closed my office door, and coldly informed me my services were no longer needed.

I was stunned and totally lost for words.

Prior to this fateful day, there had been no warnings from my superiors. No write ups. No displeasure expressed about my performance.

Nothing.

Now, after a five minute meeting, I was asked to leave the premises...*and* to be careful the door didn't hit me on my rear end on the way out.

I felt a deep sense of emptiness as I slowly made my way to the parking lot through my department of twenty people.

No one knew what was happening.

Someone actually approached me in the hallway to help resolve a problem. *"Sorry"*, I replied, *"but you'll have to see Ron about that. I've just been let go."*

I felt numb during my fifteen minute commute home. I drove in silence.

It was a bright, sunny August day. Kids were out riding their bikes and the golf course was full of people. The golfers sure looked successful, relaxed, and prosperous. I envied them.

As I approached my home, my wife, Beth, was just pulling out of the driveway.

Great timing.

During my humbling drive home I had rehearsed in my mind how I was going to tell Beth. Telling her in the middle of the street with her car window rolled down was not one of those scenarios.

She had a look of total surprise on her face as she exclaimed, *"What are you doing home?!"* I tried to act calm, cool, and collected as I said, *"Well... let's go inside, Honey. I have something to tell you."*

The next morning when I awoke, I thought everything had just been a bad dream.

OK—now what?

This may sound strange, but the very next day I actually felt a slight sense of relief. Working for my Neanderthal boss had been quite stressful; plus, I was burned out from my chaotic 60-65 hour work regiment.

I should be back on my feet in no time. After all, the door swings both ways.

For the next three weeks I slept in, started an exercise routine, and enjoyed my newfound freedom. No reason to fret. I will quickly find another job and—*besides*—I deserve to kick back and take it easy for awhile.

During my three week hiatus from the trenches of gainful employment, I had plenty of time to think about everything that led up to my firing.

I began to harbor feelings of guilt.

I should have done something to prevent this. Now I've let my beautiful family down. The reality of my situation was starting to sink in and I thought...maybe it was my fault after all.

My feelings of guilt soon flipped to anger and resentment

I replayed my firing over and over again in my mind. I became increasingly upset about the way it went down. The whole thing had been terribly unjust. I deserved better. I really couldn't think of anything I could have done differently to keep my job.

I spent too much time with friends and family rehashing the events of my termination. I soon found that although my friends were sympathetic, kind, and supportive, they really couldn't do much to sooth my pain, other than listen and tell me everything would work out for the best.

By the 6 week mark of my unemployment, I felt terribly alone and discouraged.

This pain is similar to how people feel four to six weeks after the funeral of a loved one or dear friend. The pain of death is soothed somewhat during the funeral process as family and friends meet with you to share your grief. The cards, letters, phone calls, and flowers are also quite comforting and reassuring.

But soon, everyone gets back into the rhythm of their life and the vacuum left by your loss gnaws at you continually. You soon realize you have to walk this path alone. Somehow you have to muster the inner strength to heal and move on.

I prayed and waited to be rescued. To my amazement, nothing much happened.

My thoughts ran the complete gamut of human emotion. Maybe I deserved to be fired. Maybe I'm a lousy manager. I should have never left Fleetwood for that stupid Damon job. What was I thinking? I had it so good at Fleetwood. Now my career is ruined and I'm doomed to a life of mediocrity.

All of my faults and flaws were front and center…like someone holding up a mirror to me. The past looked so secure and orderly, and the future looked so uncertain and bleak.

Isn't it amazing how much we define ourselves by how we earn our daily bread?

Before I was fired, people would ask me what I did for a living. I would proudly reply that I was the national sales manager of a luxury motor home company in the RV industry. My friends and family were always fascinated and interested in my career.

Luxury motor homes are awesome. Who hasn't dreamed about cruising down the open road in a beautiful motor home? Most corporate sales managers get a company car. I got a company motor home. How cool was that?

After my job loss when people asked me what I did for a living, I wanted to crawl under the table and hide. I hated telling people I was unemployed. And after I did, they would usually respond to me by saying something like…

"Sorry to hear that, Mike. [Pause] So, do you think the Cubs will make the playoffs this year?"

I got into the habit of telling people I was laid off rather than fired. Don't you think *getting laid off* conveys something beyond your control?

The truth?

I was flat fired, canned, terminated…given the golden boot. My boss didn't like me, so…

"You're fired!" …as The Donald would say.

Fired…laid off…downsized. Call it what you like. I felt like a big jellyfish bobbing around on the open sea. Someone else was in control of my livelihood and had just thrown me under the bus. And I didn't appreciate it too much.

So, where did I go from here?

The first thing I did—which turned out to be the *best* course of action—**was make finding a job my full time job.** I got up early in the morning, showered and dressed just as if I was going to work at a Fortune 500 company. At precisely 7:00 AM, I went into my study, closed the door, and went to work. My title: chief job seeker.

7 months of job hunting with no success...or so I thought

Despite a constant feeling of malaise, seven months into my job search, it dawned on me that my job loss had actually been a gift. Yes…a blessing. It's funny how we interpret pain as a negative. My career was about to take an exciting new turn. I was so excited about it that I even thought about sending my ex-boss a box of chocolates with a thank you note!

I'm eager to share with you why—and more importantly—what I learned along the way that will help you break through your job brick wall. I'm convinced the best days of your career are still ahead of you…regardless of your age, job history, or shortcomings.

Let me show you how to set yourself up so your next career opportunity finds you.

Where is your job loss pointing you?

Write down your job loss story. This is an important step in the healing process. Even if you feel you've gotten over how you lost your job, you will benefit by doing this exercise. It's not enough to verbalize your story to someone, or just keep it to yourself.

Follow these guidelines in writing your story:

1. Don't worry about spelling, correct grammar, or other writing dos and don'ts. Just let it flow out of you in a conversational way.

2. Type out your story on the computer, or an old typewriter...or hand write it on a legal pad, piece of stationary, napkin, papyrus, or animal skins. Use whatever writing system that best allows your feelings and emotions to flow out of you. Some people can best express how they are feeling through a pencil moving over a piece of paper. Others like to pound on the keys of an old typewriter. Do whatever works for you. Same goes for your writing implement... pencil, fountain pen, ballpoint, quill, chisel and hammer...*whatever*. The important thing is that you're comfortable and not distracted by how you record your job loss story.

3. Write your story in a quiet place where you won't be disturbed or interrupted. Early mornings can be a great time because you're refreshed and your brain has been recharged. Also, the stresses of yesterday are less intense. But you could be a night owl and most creative and motivated burning the midnight oil. If you get writers block at your favorite time, try switching to mornings or nights. This exercise is about change and closure. During this process be alert for game changing ideas and inspiration. Just try it and see what unfolds.

4. Spend about one to two hours writing your story, but it's perfectly OK to take a few hours longer…or even a day longer. Documenting your experience will help bring you closure and set you up to move on. There is therapeutic value in writing down your feelings.

5. Keep your story for future reference. After you create it, read it a couple of times, then file it away. Don't throw it away. Read it a year from now...3 years from now...*5 years from now*. After your crisis has passed and you're back into the rhythm of your life, you'll read your job loss story and learn something new about yourself. You won't believe me now, but three, five, or ten years from now, you'll actually see how your job loss turned out to be the best thing for you. You'll know exactly what I mean later. Trust me on this one. Perhaps your children and grandchildren will read your story someday and find fresh courage to face one of their own trials because of your example.

OK...enough said. Get to writing. Meet me back here when you're done.

How did your writing go? Do you feel a little better? Did you learn something about yourself?

Good.

OK...now for some good news.

Your next job is out there patiently waiting for you.

We just have to find it.

There is a company out there that desperately needs your unique gifts and talents. Some of your best friends and co-workers—who you haven't even met yet—are also waiting for you.

If you're single, perhaps the love of your life is waiting for you, feeling just as incomplete as you do right now.

So, let's put this unemployment thing behind us and get on with the finer things of life.

Chapter 2:
Setting Up Your Job Search Base Camp

The happiest heart that ever beat
Was in some quiet breast
That found the common daylight sweet,
And left to Heaven the rest.
~John Vance Cheney

Find a place in your home or apartment where you can *go to work* every day. Make this space special and personal to you. I realize you may have limited space, but you'll be surprised what you can do with it.

I'll give you some good ideas in a minute, but for now I want you to understand why this is so important.

Job hunting is hard work.

You're not going to want to do it...especially if you've been looking a long time, and you're sick and tired of all the rejection and BS you've had to put up with.

If you do your job search at the same computer desk where all your overdue bills are staring up at you, or your desk is a mess, or if you've been wasting time at your computer playing video games...what kind of mindset are you going to have when you really need to knuckle down and make something happen?

Your work space is—*well*—your place of work. All of your notes, tools, and materials should be there waiting for you each day. This makes it easier for you to pick up where you left off yesterday, and to do something productive rather than constantly fumbling around to find things.

Ideally, your work space should be a warm, inviting place.

Here are some ideas on how to organize your work space from the ideal set-up, to working out of a tiny studio apartment, or even a rented room.

Regardless of how opulent or humble your current circumstances, *everyone* needs to comply with these minimum requirements:

- **Work from a clean desk or table.** Any papers, books, magazines, notes, bills, plates, cups, forks, folders, hand tools, remote controls, gum wrappers, or other clutter needs to be put away, thrown away, or given away. When all of this stuff is gone and out of sight, completely wipe down, clean, and polish your desk or table—same thing with your computer. Your work space should look good, smell good, and feel good.

- **Make sure your work space has good lighting.** The best light comes from a desk lamp close to your work surface with a plain old incandescent light bulb. You want your work space illuminated with a warm, pleasant light.

- **Remove anything from your room or space that is distracting, unsightly, or inappropriate.**

  - Stacks of books or newspapers

  - Piles of clothing

  - Dusty, uninspiring pictures on the walls with no meaning to you

  - Windows with fingerprints or oily film on them

  - Cock-eyed window blinds with an inch-and-a-half of dust on them

  - Beat-up television

  - Walls that haven't seen a fresh coat of paint since the War of 1812

Pearl of Wisdom: You might be asking yourself: *"What do these mundane, simple things have to do with my job search?"*

Plenty!

How do you feel about your car when it's showroom clean and polished inside and out? It even rides better...*right?*

How do you feel about yourself when you get your hair done and put on some stylish new clothes for an evening out? You didn't know you could look so good.

The same principle applies to your work space.

Don't jinx yourself by not doing this. You did come here for change, didn't you?

OK—change.

Small home or apartment with no private study or second bedroom

Set up a small desk in your bedroom in the best corner. If you don't have a desk, you can buy an inexpensive card table at Wal-Mart for $30 to $40, or Goodwill for $10. You don't even need to buy a chair because you can use one of your kitchen table chairs.

Why not your living room or dining room?

Because you need a private place to retreat where you can close the door and *go to work*. You don't need *any* distractions during your job search time. You need to be laser focused. The idea is to isolate yourself and signal to everyone in your household—including your cat and/or dog—that when you're working...Do Not Disturb. Even if you're single, it's a change of pace and will help you get out of your routine and into the mindset of job hunting.

What about my computer?

Relax. We'll get to that in a minute.

If your bedroom is really tiny, move your bed and dresser around to see if you can somehow create a workspace. If it barely fits, but you can't really walk around very well, set up your table when you have a one or two hour time block to work, and simply take it down when you're done.

On the wall in front of your temporary work space, put up an inspiring picture or poster of a beach, garden, forest, family gathering, sailboats, or any other special place, person, or thing. Positive visuals will uplift you and *fill you with delight.*

Keep all of your job notes and information in a notebook and/or a portable accordion file folder. This way when you're ready to go to work, just set up your card table, plunk your warm light on your table, tape up your pictures/poster, scoop up your notebook and accordion folder, grab your portable phone or cell phone—*and*—you're in business.

Pearl of Wisdom: Every once in awhile, put some fresh flowers on your desk. Yes, even if you're a guy. We are visual creatures. Looking at natural beauty makes us feel connected with forces outside of ourselves. It can be comforting and calming as we steadily push forward. Surround yourself with positive, attractive things and your attitude is likely to follow.

Mike's Rant: Some people will blow this off as nonsense—hope you're not one of them. Let me ask you a question. Do you feel any different eating lunch in a quaint restaurant vs. chowing down on a burger at McDonalds? Why? In both places your hunger is being satisfied. So, what's the difference?

Do you feel any different running on a treadmill vs. jogging through a lush green forest with birds serenading you as you run?

Why? You're getting your exercise in either place.

*Bottom line...*you will be twice as motivated to get busy with your job search if your work environment is pleasant and positive. Job hunting is hard work. Creating the right environment and using a good job search strategy will lift your spirits, and strengthen your resolve to do it.

OK...what about your computer?

It doesn't really matter where your computer is located because most of your job-search time will be spent on the telephone talking with people (a lot more on this later).

Most of your computer time will be spent doing research—not looking for jobs. Yes...you read that right. In other words, your actual work space is where you will execute your plan. It's where the rubber meets the road.

Twenty percent of your time should be spent researching on the computer, and 80 percent of your time should be spent networking with people.

You'll be more motivated to *get to work* if you've created a pleasant work atmosphere and have a daily plan. Your computer is a good tool, but it can also be a distraction and time waster.

Thriving in a chaotic or depressing home environment

Does one of the following annoying people reside at or within ear shot of your home?

- Unsupportive, pushy, needy spouse

- Critical, negative, overbearing, needy parent(s)

- Inconsiderate, self-centered, sloppy, loud roommate

- Rough and tumble, whiny, spoiled kids

- Noisy neighbors

- Demanding pets who crave attention and think they own the place

- Nearby businesses with a paging system

- Sirens, trains rumbling down the tracks, or aircraft taking off or landing near your house

If your home environment is a complete zoo, you need to find a place outside of your home to go about your job search. An ideal place to start is your local public library.

Most libraries are centrally located within easy reach by bus, bike, car, or foot. You won't be able to make phone calls to prospective employers in the library, but you can do your research and put your call list together in peace and quiet.

If you haven't been to your library in awhile, make it a point to visit soon. You'll be pleasantly surprised. Most libraries are modern, up to date, inviting, comfortable places to work and think. Also, don't be bashful about asking the librarians to acquaint you with all of the job hunting resources they have available.

Thanks to the Great Recession of 2009, many libraries have extensive job hunting resources. Librarians *love* to help people. Most of them know a ton about where to find stuff.

In some libraries you will have *free* access to expensive online databases ($1,000-$2,500 annual subscription fee if you had to purchase on your own). Also, they may even allow you to access their databases from your home computer using your library card number. This is possible even in my small community library.

Some libraries may even have Wi-Fi access if you have a laptop, and comfortable chairs and tables to work at.

Pearl of Wisdom: You are *always* employed even if you aren't drawing a paycheck at the moment. Set up a daily work schedule, and tell everyone in your home when you will be gone during your *working hours*. No exceptions. If you were gainfully employed, you would be required to be at your company post during work hours. Why should this time in your life be any different?

If one of your family members complains about it (usually because they are only thinking of their needs, not yours), calmly tell them you have a job training meeting or a pre-job interview preparation meeting you must attend. This meeting, of course, is with yourself, but this usually satisfies them and you can now *go to work*.

I'm not suggesting you lie to your family or other important people in your life. But if they don't respect you enough to give you the space you need to find a job, then you just need to handle them a little differently to protect your time.

OK...how are you suppose to network with people or make follow up calls with prospective employers from the library?

Well, you can't.

And—we already know you can't do this at home with your kids scream-ing, the dog constantly barking, and your goofy neighbor revving up his Harley in his driveway.

Suggestions on where to make your phone calls:

- Explain your circumstances to a close friend or relative. Ask if you can make calls from a room in their home. It's possible they could even give you access to their home or apartment while they're at work.

- Make calls from your car, parked in your driveway or another safe location—free from noise and distractions.

- Ask a close friend, relative, or acquaintance if their place of business has a spare office or room you can use. You'd be surprised how many accountants, lawyers, and other business people have extra space they're not using. If you can't think of anyone to approach about this, ask your minister, rabbi, or priest if they know anyone who might be open to helping you. Ask if they will introduce you to them.

- Speaking of your clergy, maybe a room at your church, synagogue, or mosque could be made available to you.

- Sometimes churches host job networking groups that hold daily or weekly meetings. Attend one of these meetings and ask others for ideas as to where you can go to make calls and follow up on leads. Sometimes three or four people meet together a couple of times a week to make follow up or prospecting calls at the same time. Studies have shown that you will make more calls if you are in a support group. Some groups even make a game out of it and challenge each other to make a minimum number of calls an hour. Simply put...you might feel more accountable and motivated do-ing it this way; therefore, you'll make more calls and get better results.

True story: Job seeker does phone interview from her closet

I know a very successful sales trainer who was out of work and looking for a job. She had three small children at home who were constantly tugging on her, spilling things, squealing or crying. She lived in a small apartment in New York City.

During the day she could sometimes make a handful of calls during nap time...if she was lucky enough to get the kids to doze off without her collapsing herself. In the evenings, she just couldn't get away because of the demands of her family.

Fortunately, her husband provided her with some relief by watching their kids; but, despite his help, the atmosphere was still pretty noisy and distracting for her to confidently make a brief follow up call, or participate in a phone interview with a serious employer.

So, Heidi came up with a crazy idea that actually paid off because she landed a *very* good job.

Heidi would actually do a phone interview or make networking calls in her closet. You know...shoes and all. I am not making this up! She would go into her bedroom, lock the door, crawl into her closet, and shut the door.

Viola!—instant office.

She could still hear muffled cries, occasional crashes, and chaos, but the person on the other end of the line thought her home was a perfect place of peace and harmony. Sometimes her kids would even thump on the bedroom door until her husband would fetch them.

By the way...two years later Heidi shared her story with me and her new employer at a company convention during happy hour. We all laughed and roasted her about it. But it would have been no laughing matter had she tried to pull off her interview in the heat of battle with her kids bouncing off the walls.

The best way to stay organized so nothing slips through the cracks

News Flash: Paper and pen are still necessary and are never going away.

Even if you are a highly organized person, don't skip over this short section. Surprisingly, one of the reasons you may not be getting job interviews is because you are either *too* organized or *too* laid back.

I have found that there are two types of people who seem to have the most trouble with their job search routine:

1. The terminally unorganized

2. The super organized.

The *terminals* struggle because they lack a consistent, systematic approach to finding a job. They fly by the seat of their pants and often have a one-dimensional job hunting approach...usually applying to online Internet ads. They then proceed to light a candle, say a prayer, and hope someone with hiring authority calls them soon.

Important contact information often falls through the cracks, and they fumble around when someone calls to set up an interview because they usually don't remember sending them a resume. How embarrassing.

At the other end of the spectrum are the *super organized*...the neat freaks. They have a chart and graph for everything in a PDF, Word, and/or Excel format. They spend hours tweaking and rewriting their resume and scouring the internet for job leads.

Trouble is...most of their day is spent tweaking and organizing, not making calls to folks who can either hire them, or direct them to someone who can.

The secret to an effective job search routine is...

Keep it simple.

JibberJobber: A tool to organize your job search and manage your career

One of the best ways to manage your job search is through an online tool called JibberJobber (http://www.jibberjobber.com). JibberJobber is an online career management tool developed by Jason Alba in 2006. After you've finished reading this chapter, you can learn all about it by visiting his website. The best place to start is the video introduction on their home page.

When you first start your job search, keeping track of job leads, referrals, and where you send your resume is pretty simple. It doesn't matter if you use a spiral notebook, legal pad, or even floating pieces of paper.

It's easy to remember the jobs you applied for and where you sent your resume. After a week of job hunting, things get a little more hectic, but you still can find your notes—kind of like the junk in your top dresser drawer.

Fast forward one month.

This is when it dawns on most folks that they really don't have a very organized way to keep track of their job search activities.

You might even experience this embarrassing moment:

Caller: Hello...is this Suzie Q?

You: Yes it is.

Caller: This is Ben Dover calling from Crash-a-Lot Computers.

You: Um...OK...err...What is this about?

Caller: You sent us your resume last month.

You: Oh...yeah...right...RIGHT! [Sounds of papers shuffling]

Caller: Are you still available and is this a good time to talk?

You:	Yeah...sure. [As you spit out your gum] What did you say your name was?
Caller:	Ben Dover, the HR Manager.
You:	And...um...What was the name of your company again? Sorry.
Caller:	Crash-a-Lot Computers.
You:	Hang on a minute while I check my notes [As your frantically rummage around trying to figure out why you sent them your resume].
Caller:	Did I call you at a bad time?
You:	No...NO! I just need to...hold on a sec...OK here it is...

This is exactly what will happen if you don't have some kind of a system that helps you pinpoint everyone you've called, mailed a resume to, or emailed—and why. When one of the most important calls of your life comes in, you need to be prepared.

You might be saying to yourself: I'm pretty organized and even use a nifty Excel spreadsheet with all my stuff on it.

JibberJobber is ten times better than a spreadsheet and even has hyperlinks to job descriptions, websites, and other crucial information. Best of all, JibberJobber is free because most job seekers are on a tight budget and a diet of Raman Noodles.

Once your career is back on solid ground, JibberJobber now becomes your career management tool since most people will change jobs every three to five years.

Depressing thought, isn't it?

JibberJobber even works in tandem with your social networking sites like LinkedIn, Twitter, and Facebook. So, you won't be duplicating your efforts. We'll be talking about how social networking ties in with your job search later in the book.

Despite the usefulness of JibberJobber, you still need a place to jot down notes and other important information when you're talking with people on the phone. I use a yellow legal pad. In other words, when you're in the heat of battle, don't worry about how best to organize things. Just take notes and sort it out later. Using a legal pad is much better than jotting things down on floating pieces of paper.

Later in the book I'll share with you some calling scripts and good questions to ask. Regardless, during your call blocks you want to connect with as many people as possible. Pen and paper is still the best way to jot down important information on the fly.

You can organize to your heart's content after you've made a bunch of calls. You're not going to find a job if all you do is slice and dice information or spend half your day thrashing around trying to find an important phone number.

In the next chapter we're going to talk about specific habits, behaviors, and boundaries you need to develop to put you firmly on the path to employment.

Chapter 3:
Ten Simple Habits of Highly Successful Job Seekers

Meet the sun every morning as if it could cast a ballot.
~Henry Cabot Lodge Jr.

For the next twenty-one days, you are most likely to experience a breakthrough in your job search if you stick to the following daily regiment:

1. Early to rise...your first private victory of the day

Getting off to an early start will give you confidence and a sense of accomplishment, even if your day doesn't yield any measurable results. At least you can lay your head down that night knowing you put your best foot forward.

Start your day *no later than* 6:30 AM, Monday through Friday.

There are fewer distractions and interruptions in the morning. The phone isn't ringing. No one is knocking on your door. No one is making demands on you. It's quieter and more peaceful.

This quiet time allows you to gather your thoughts and plan your day.

However, you're not going to spring out of bed in the morning with glee if you stayed up the night before watching Jay Leno, or some other mindless TV show. Make sure you go to bed at a reasonable hour—like 10:30 PM—to allow yourself seven to eight hours of sleep a night.

There have been numerous studies done on how much sleep is really necessary. Scientific research confirms that most people need seven to nine hours of sleep a night to function optimally, and feel good the next day.

The late great football coach, Vince Lombardi, once said, *"Fatigue makes cowards of us all."*

Did you also know that your immune system functions at only 50 percent if you are tired, worn out, and sleep deprived?

Pearl of Wisdom: You are very vulnerable right now. Your emotions and feelings have the power to either motivate you, or paralyze you. Getting off to an early start requires effort and self-discipline. When you're down, you feel tired and withdrawn. Everything is a major effort. When you're in charge of yourself, your emotions and thoughts naturally follow suit. It is easier to shrug off rejection and keep moving forward. So, your first accomplishment of the day is rolling out of bed at 6:30 AM. Let's go—and don't tell me you're not a morning person.

---

2. Dress for success

Shower, groom, and dress just like you would if you were headed out the door for work.

No more sitting at your desk in your pajamas with a serious case of bed head slurping on a cup of coffee. The first time you *dress for success* expect someone in your family to turn their head in astonishment and say, *"Where are you going today?!"*

If you get this kind of reaction, you're on the right track.

If you are single, still follow this dress code. When you look your best, you'll feel good about yourself and will go about your day with greater determination and confidence.

Pearl of Wisdom: How you dress also makes an emotional connection with your soul mate and other family members who depend on you. You communicate to them in a powerful, non-verbal way that *you mean business* about finding a job.

Your dependents are suffering and worried, too.

When they see you getting up early and putting on your *work uniform*, it conveys to them that you love them and you'll do *whatever it takes* to provide for them.

In return, you will earn their respect, support, and affection during one of your down spells.

When your loved ones respond to you this way, you will recover faster. It will be 10 times easier to climb back up in the saddle and keep driving forward.

The downward spiral that you've endured all these months will reverse course, and the upward spiral will begin to gain momentum.

---

3. You are what you eat

Eat something healthy for breakfast.

You might be saying to yourself, *"I don't eat breakfast."* Well now is a good time to start a healthy new habit.

Countless studies have concluded that the most important meal of the day is breakfast. It provides energy for both your mind and body. All you need is a small bowl of cereal sprinkled with raisins or fruit. By 9:00 AM, you'll experience a noticeable surge of energy and alertness.

Just do it.

This extra shot of adrenalin could give you the courage to make one more phone call or follow up with someone *just this one last time* resulting in a breakthrough.

In the end, it's often the little things that make all the difference.

4. The news isn't the news...it's the bad news

Do not turn on the TV or read the newspaper first thing in the morning—too many negatives. You simply can't afford to expose yourself to any sad, depressing, unfortunate stories or situations right now.

Reading or watching this stuff won't help you, but it certainly has wet blanket power.

Avoid it like the plague.

Pearl of Wisdom: When we are falling short of our expectations and feeling down about ourselves, watching the news actually gives us a sugar high. We feel better about ourselves when someone else is worse off than we are, or suffering more.

If the economy is screwed up, or unemployment is getting worse, we then conclude that it is not our fault because, *"no one is hiring."* Pretty soon we get lulled to sleep with this kind of thinking—and take less action because what's the use in trying?

This is a trap. Stay away from extremes in your thinking.

Put yourself in a positive environment and you will attract positive energy and feelings. The momentum will start to build in your favor.

---

5. Read something positive, inspiring, uplifting

First thing in the morning, take ten minutes to feed your mind with positive thoughts and impressions. The ideal time to do this is while you are eating your breakfast.

If you're not sure what to read, take time today or tomorrow (don't delay!) to visit your local library or bookstore. Most large bookstores have entire sections focusing on self-help or personal development. Spend an hour or two browsing through books until you find something that speaks to you.

Watching a video or listening to an audio presentation on your computer is OK once in awhile. But hefting a book in your hands, turning the pages, highlighting, underlining, or writing down some notes in the margins is more empowering.

10 books with the power to awaken the giant within you:

1. *100 Ways to Motivate Yourself*, by Steve Chandler

2. *His Needs, Her Needs, Building an Affair-Proof Marriage,* by Willard F. Harley Jr.

3. *Chicken Soup for the Soul*, by Jack Canfield and Mark Victor Hansen

4. *First Things First*, by Stephen R. Covey

5. *The 7 Habits of Highly Effective People,* by Stephen R. Covey

6. *What Color is Your Parachute?* by Richard N. Bolles

7. *Man's Search for Meaning*, by Victor E. Frankl

8. *God Never Blinks: 50 Lessons for Life's Little Detours,* by Regina Brett

9. *Think and Grow Rich!: The Original Version, Restored and Revised*, by Napoleon Hill

10. *Who Moved My Cheese?* By Spencer Johnson, Kenneth Blanchard

Note: You can purchase these books from Amazon through my website. Go to: http://www.job-interview-wisdom.com/life-changing-books.html.

Pearls of Wisdom: I'm always dismayed when someone tells me they don't like to read, and thus deny themselves rich treasures of wisdom that can be found nowhere else.

The greatest invention of all time was the printing press.

Reading is exercise for the mind. Reading is also a form of work as you have to use your imagination and reasoning skills to process information.

You can actually increase your intelligence by reading.

The wisdom of many of the greatest thinkers who have ever graced our planet is recorded in print for everyone to benefit. For just ten minutes a day you can tap into this reservoir of knowledge and become aware of life-changing ideas.

So, while you're munching on your cereal in the morning and filling your stomach, fill your mind and soul with nourishment, too.

Picture this pleasant scene in your mind. It's 6:30 AM. Your home is quiet and not a creature is stirring. As you wipe the sleepy stuff out of your eyes and get dressed, your mind is free to wander without distractions or interruptions. Yesterdays problems have faded.

You spend the next twenty minutes in silence, eating your breakfast while supping from the pages of an inspiring book. For this short time you are immersed in a positive environment and preparing yourself to embrace the opportunities of the day.

You still will have some down days—but hopefully fewer than before.

Later we're going to talk about what you can do when you are so depressed you can hardly roll out of bed. We're also going to talk about getting punched in the stomach with rejection or some other unexpected setback.

6. Slow down...be a tortoise

Yes, you read that right. I want you to s-l-o-w d-o-w-n. I'm sure you're familiar with the saying, "haste makes waste." Well, it's true, and it especially applies to your job search.

When you learn how to swim, one of the first things you are taught is to relax in the water. Usually, on your very first lesson, your instructor will get you to lie on your back in the water while they gently support you. It's pretty amazing that with very little movement, and only 10% of your body weight being supported by your instructor that you actually float... and don't sink straight to the bottom of the pool.

Compare this peaceful floating scene to someone who is drowning. What do you witness? Pure panic—arms flailing, legs kicking, and someone struggling with all of their energy to keep their head above water.

Oddly enough, all this effort almost always results in the person drowning.

This same principle applies to learning how to fly. The first time a student pilot is handed the controls of an airplane they almost always grab the controls with both hands in a vise grip. The harder they try to control the airplane, the more it pitches up or down, and the less control the student pilot has.

A good flight instructor will usually say to the student pilot, *"Just let go of all the controls and see what happens."* Most students exclaim, *"You want me to let go?! Won't the plane crash?!"*

The instructor will calmly reply, *"Well...let go of the controls and let's find out."*

When the student lets go of the controls, the plane practically flies itself. The instructor will then have the student fly the airplane with one finger. If the nose of the airplane pitches up slightly, just push on the yoke with one finger until it is level again. Same thing applies if the nose pitches down. Pull up slightly with one finger until the plane is level.

After about ten minutes of flying the airplane with one finger the wise flight instructor usually says something like this to the student pilot: *"Ninety percent of the flying is done by the airplane, and 10 percent of the flying is done by you."*

This same principle applies to your job search.

You need to s-l-o-w d-o-w-n and go about your job search in a systematic, balanced way to leverage your odds of getting interviews and ultimately winning a job offer.

In short, there is a rhythm to a successful job search and we're trying to find your groove.

However, the longer people are out of work, the more *low result* activities they try like:

- Shot-gunning out hundreds of resumes to recruiters and companies
- Scouring the internet for job postings
- Repeatedly calling companies and recruiters after you've sent them your resume and asking, *"Do you have anything for me?"*

Panic sets in resulting in unnecessary grief, anxiety, depression, and the mistaken belief that there are no jobs out there, or worse yet, no one wants you because you're damaged goods.

Hopefully, over the next few days, I'll convince you otherwise. But for now, were going to slow down and move forward in an organized, systematic, step-by-step fashion.

7. Escape to your special private place when you're discouraged or unmotivated

In another life, I worked for someone who treated me with indifference. This person didn't like me for some strange reason, so he basically ignored me and only spoke to me when he had to. This is classic passive-aggressive behavior. And it was hurtful to me.

Who doesn't want to feel valued, needed, and respected?

One day, I was having a stressful day. Nothing was going right. My manager said something to me very deflating and inappropriate. The intention was clearly to hurt me.

Since my boss had power over me, there was nothing I could do about it. Even so, I felt he had crossed the line this time. I almost resigned on the spot.

After my boss left my office, I became so upset about it that I said to myself, *"I've got to get out of here or I'm going to say or do something I'll regret."*

Behind our office complex is a large field with a beautiful grove of tall oak and pine trees. It is a peaceful, secluded place. There is a short access road to the trees with just a flimsy gate. The trees are not visible from our offices as all our windows face in the opposite direction.

I decided to leave the office and take a short walk back to the trees just to be alone for twenty to thirty minutes. It was a beautiful summer morning. The short walk did me good. When I arrived at the trees I walked a short distance into the grove.

I just stood there...*and listened*.

I heard crickets chirping, birds singing, and gentle breezes blowing through the trees. In this peaceful environment, everything was in harmony with nature and working perfectly.

I said a short prayer and asked for strength.

I felt a divine connection. It was soothing to my soul. I just stood there, and drank it all in for the next twenty minutes. My feelings of anger and frustration slowly subsided.

I walked back to my office and resumed my day, leaving my burdens of anger and frustration back in the woods.

Did you watch the 2010 Vancouver Winter Olympics?

USA Olympian Apolo Ohno added to his metal collection in speed skating, making him the most decorated American Winter Olympic athlete of all time.

Did you know that at Apolo's first Olympic trial—despite being judged a heavy favorite—he finished dead last? After this humiliating setback, Apolo decided to quit speed skating.

Apolo's father—aware of his son's great athletic potential and the temporary nature of his setback—took him to a remote cabin on a Washington beach. He instructed his son to remain there alone until he figured out what he wanted to do with his life.

A week later, Apolo contacted his father and told him he wanted to skate.

Apolo's solitude also healed deep wounds between him and his father as their relationship was strained. Today they are very close...a triumph much greater than any athletic pursuit or honor.

On those rare days when you feel an overwhelming sense of confusion and discouragement, stop what you're doing. Take a short time-out from life and go to your special private place in nature. In this peaceful setting, you will find solace and renewed energy to continue your journey.

Special Tip: There may be times where you simply can't go to your special private place. But your special place is still available and waiting for you.

It's within you.

Simply lie down on a sofa, or sit in a comfortable chair. Close your eyes, breathe slowly, and go to your special place in your mind for ten to fifteen minutes.

Imagine the sights, sounds, smells, and feelings of that place. It's not as good as actually being there, but you will still benefit from this experience.

8. Do not spend every waking hour job hunting and obsessing about your job search

It's true...you need a job in the worst way right now. So, shouldn't you spend every waking hour, turning over every rock, to find a one?

No

Look at your job search as a marathon, not a sprint. For best results, act more like a tortoise instead of a jackrabbit.

This approach helps you avoid burnout, depression, and procrastination. Once these negative emotions creep into your life, you will take less and less action, and become more and more complacent and unmotivated.

Worse yet, these emotions can become so painful that good people often embrace bad habits to try and fill the gaping hole in their heart.

Some bummed out job seekers will:

- Drink more and start drinking earlier in the day

- Stay up too late at night, and then try to get through the day on four hours of sleep

- Watch too much TV

- Sleep more than is needful

- Snack all day long

- Nap during the day

- Play video games or aimlessly surf the net

- Tidy up the garage or work on the car...any excuse to avoid job hunting

- Go overboard on personal fitness.

You may already be at this stage and harbor a lot of guilt about it. But, just as easily as you can drift into a few bad habits, you can form good ones.

Studies show that it takes about three weeks to form a new habit.

But, the really good news is that within a day or two of your new routine, you *will* start to feel more optimistic and motivated…even if you experience a brief relapse. The reason for this shift in attitude is your renewed self-discipline.

Pearl of Wisdom: Ever wonder how bad habits get started in the first place? It boils down to two things: Pain and Pleasure. Our DNA is programmed to avoid pain and seek pleasure.

Whenever our pain gets too intense, we try to find ways to relieve our suffering. Unfortunately, many of the pleasures we embrace are short-lived, and often leave us feeling guilty and unfulfilled.

One way to interrupt this pattern and move to higher ground, is to embrace a new regiment like this program. This forces you to alter your daily routines and to think and act in new ways. One small private victory has the power to rejuvenate you and move you forward. Pretty soon, momentum kicks in like a swift current, and you wonder how you ever got sidetracked.

Action Step: Here is an exercise to help you get outside of yourself when you feel discouraged. Write down all of your current roles in life. These might include, father, mother, husband, wife, son, daughter, brother, sister, grandparent, provider, homemaker, volunteer, friend, neighbor, missionary, teacher, writer, Scout leader, club member, and others.

Keep your list in a place where you can easily refer to it each day. As you begin your day, look at all of your roles and ask yourself: *What is one thing I can do today to make a difference in one or more of these important roles?*

They don't have to be major tasks either. Here are a few suggestions:

- Call someone out of the blue to see how things are going, expecting nothing in return.

- Attend a local job networking meeting to provide support to other struggling job seekers.

- Meet someone for breakfast or lunch.

- Ask your spouse/significant-other out on a date. Make it a weekly habit.

- Volunteer for a service project at your church or in your community.

True Story

Jim didn't like his job as a Financial Adviser for a major insurance company. His job required fifty-five to sixty hour work weeks including evenings and Saturdays. Jim's work-life balance was out of whack and taking a toll on his family.

Despite his demanding schedule, Jim looked for another job with minimal success. He felt trapped, discouraged, and lost.

One Saturday his church was doing a short service project at the chapel in the morning and asked Jim if he could help. Just what Jim needed, more time away from his wife and kids. For some reason, he couldn't say no. After all, it was only a couple of hours. Besides, he liked the people he was going to be hanging out with.

So, off Jim went to the service project. At the end of this short event, Jim met briefly with his friend Rick, who just happened to have a great job as Purchasing Manager with a major local manufacturer.

They talked about non-work related stuff when, out of the blue, Rick asked Jim how his job was going. Jim told him his situation and said he was actively looking to make a change. To Jim's amazement, Rick then proceeded to tell him that his company was looking for a Sales Rep. He invited Jim to have lunch with him on Monday and take a tour of the plant.

To make a long story short, Jim met Rick for lunch, took the plant tour, and when it was over, Rick introduced him to his General Manager. An interview was scheduled with the GM and a week later Jim was offered the job. He accepted and went on to enjoy a long and satisfying career with this company. Jim had absolutely no clue any of this would happen by simply attending a church service project.

What does all this have to do with your job search?

Often times when we set aside our troubles for a brief time and focus on others, opportunities find us. Most of our blessings in life come by way of other people. Sometimes we are the givers and sometimes we are the receivers in this process. Either way, everyone benefits.

Eventually what goes around comes around.

9. Follow promptings...even illogical ones

Open your mind and consider all of your job options. You need to look at things from a fresh perspective and be as open minded and flexible as possible.

The only thing for sure right now is *nothing is for sure*.

Let's say you've decided not to relocate. One day, out of the blue, a friend calls you with a *dream-come-true* job lead. Only one problem...the job is five hundred miles away in South Dakota, of all places. Instead of immediately rejecting this lead, what have you got to lose by exploring it?

If this lead turns into a job offer, you can always turn it down. No one has a gun to your head. Let's continue this relocation example a bit further to see how you might benefit from this off-the-wall job lead.

Most job seekers today prefer *not* to relocate for some of the following logical reasons:

- Kids in high school

- Home values are too low

- Upside down in their mortgage

- Watching over an elderly parent

- Kids love their sports or other activities

- The weather, culture, or lifestyle of an area

- Extended family lives in the area

- Grew up there and have never relocated

- Lots of friends and ties to a community

- Enjoy their church stewardship

These are all *very* legitimate reasons not to move. **However**, if you've been unemployed for months on end with no job prospects on the horizon, you need to step back and ask yourself: *How long can I go without a job before I hit the wall?*

You may be in love with your location, but if you can't find work after months of trying, you need to consider every option under the sun to shake something loose, *including moving*.

Even if you are **adamant** about not moving...please keep reading.

If you're a person of faith, I'm sure you've spent many days and nights praying in earnest for God to help you find a job. Perhaps your faith has even been shaken to the core because it doesn't seem like God is answering your prayers.

Have you considered the possibility that God may have a calling for you elsewhere?

Maybe one of your children needs to be in a particular environment to reach their full potential.

Maybe someone you've never met needs you. Maybe God is leading you to a specific place for a special purpose, but the only way to get your attention is to say *no* to your prayer to find a local job.

Perhaps your pain right now is actually an *answer* to your prayers, but you're not interpreting it that way. Often times we make major decisions based on our limited logic instead of following a prompting and exercising faith.

Here is another way to determine whether or not you are *supposed to* relocate. Set a *deadline* in your quest to find a local job.

Make this commitment to yourself and to God:

"Over the next sixty days, I'm going to pull out all the stops and do everything in my power to find a local job. I'm going to pray for help. On the sixtieth day, if nothing promising is happening, I'm going to expand my search to within a two hundred mile radius of our home. If that doesn't yield any results after thirty days of looking, I will expand the radius of my search to five hundred miles. If still no results after another thirty days, I'm going to look for a job from sea to shining sea. In the interim, my heart and mind will remain open to job leads or other promptings that may be calling out to me."

Pearl of Wisdom: In each and every job interview, you have the power to say yes or no to a job offer. But if you don't get an offer, you have no options. Trust your instincts and feelings. If you are spiritually in tune, you will receive a powerful witness of what you're supposed to do.

True Story

Wes and his family enjoyed the good life in Wisconsin. They liked everything about Wisconsin—the Midwest values, good schools, affordable housing, wonderful friends, and the Green Bay Packers. Despite their comfortable lifestyle, a wonderful job opportunity for Wes came along in southwest Michigan.

After a lot of prayer and soul searching, Wes and his family reluctantly moved to Michigan. It was a difficult move and shortly after arriving they wondered if they had made the right decision. They deeply missed their Wisconsin home.

One day their young son was diagnosed with a rare form of autism. They were devastated by the news. Just so happens that the leading specialist in the United States for this rare form of autism had his clinic twenty miles from their new home. Their son made remarkable progress under this doctor's care and received the exact treatment he needed.

Do you suppose the divine hand of providence had anything to do with this?

Many people who have been unemployed for many months eventually arrive at a point where they simply do not know what to do. When your job search literally hits a brick wall, it can be frightening. Discouragement turns to depression, then to fear, and finally *panic* sets in.

Nothing seems to make sense anymore. You question everything and doubt yourself at every turn. Your mind creates images of the worst possible outcomes: living with relatives, homelessness, bankruptcy, and some people even contemplate suicide.

But...it's often at this low point in your life that a door opens. Fear and pain carries with it the benefit of pushing us in a direction we wouldn't naturally pursue on our own.

Have you ever noticed how great turning points in history are always preceded by periods of profound crisis and confusion?

Let's go back in history and compare the state of humanity just prior to:

- The Renaissance (the Dark Ages)

- Invention of printing press (ignorance, illiteracy, lost treasures of knowledge)

- The Industrial Revolution (isolated agrarian culture with a weak middle class)

- Declaration of Independence (limited freedoms and wealth opportunities)

- Birth of democracy (feudal system/dictators)

- Women's rights (second class citizenship for women)

- Abolition (slavery, Civil War)

- Quantum physics (pre-space age, pre-nuclear age)

- The economic boom of the 1950s and 1960s (Great Depression, WW2)

This pattern is telling us that we *will* emerge from the current world-wide recession into a new era of prosperity and opportunity. I'm very optimistic. If history repeats itself, something very positive and life-changing is about to dawn.

Think what this means for us and our children.

So, when everything seems to be falling apart, and nothing seems to be going right for you, it is always a sign that something very good is about to happen. The door swings both ways.

Here is another powerful example:

Are you familiar with the history of the Great Irish Potato Famine?

This was a period of mass starvation and economic collapse in Ireland between the years 1845 and 1852. Over one million people died of starvation and disease, and another million people emigrated from Ireland— dropping their overall population by 25 percent.

This huge crisis was caused by the Potato Blight, a disease that devastates potato plants. During that time, one-third of the population of Ireland depended on potatoes for their main food source—which oddly enough are native to North America.

The effects of this famine permanently changed Ireland's political, demographic, and cultural landscape, even to this day. Could anything good come from such a painful, tragic event?

Well, actually—*yes*.

Irish famine immigrants were the first wave of refugees to America. As of 2008, more than thirty-six million Americans—11.9 percent of our population—claim to have some Irish ancestry. These Irish immigrants helped shape our great nation and contributed greatly to our rich culture.

Did you know that nineteen US Presidents were of Irish descent, most notably, George Washington, Andrew Jackson, John Kennedy, Ronald Reagan, and George Bush?

You also probably know most if not all of these Irish Americans:

- Harrison Ford - Actor
- Henry Ford - Founder Ford Motor Co
- Jack Welch - Former CEO of GE
- Walt Disney
- John Ford - Movie director
- Tim Russert - Journalist
- Ed Sullivan
- Brian Williams - Journalist
- Audie Murphy - Most decorated combat soldier of WW2
- James Braddock - Champion boxer
- Tom Brady – Three time Super Bowl champion quarterback
- Eileen Collins - First female Commander of the Space Shuttle
- Davy Crockett - Pioneer, politician
- Grace Kelly - Actress
- Sandra Day O'Connor - First female Supreme Court Justice

The list of famous Irish-Americans is exhaustive. Their contributions to politics, art, entertainment, business, and literature are enormous.

So, thanks to the Irish Potato Famine, many of the ancestors of these Irish greats came to America, and played a huge role in transforming our unique culture into the envy of the world.

Where would all of us be today without the contributions of these amazing immigrants?

The reason I spent so much time on all of this is because...

Maybe you are going through your own personal potato famine and you're supposed to be somewhere else. Perhaps *major pain* is the only way to get your attention.

Your dream job and dream life could be just over the next horizon.

10. Involve your soul mate and children in your job search

It is of paramount importance that you communicate your action plan with your soul mate and children. Ask for their opinion, help and support.

Your career choice is a family affair and their lives will be impacted by your decision. Everyone needs to know what is going on, and be able to share openly with you how they feel about it.

Sometimes you'll get a lot of grief about your job possibilities, and sometimes you'll be greeted with elation and excitement. Either way, your family needs to be assured that everything is going to work out, and you only want the best for them.

Ask for their opinion and input even if you get a lot of attitude. It's human nature to fear the unknown and resist change.

How you communicate your job struggle can make a huge difference in the attitude, reaction, and support of your loved ones. They also will get a flavor of the pressure you're under and witness how you work through major life problems.

Here is a good way to involve your family in your job search. Over the next few days, you'll witness a positive, supportive change in everyone's attitude.

At the beginning of the day, tell your family that you would like to talk with them that night about something very important. Tell them you would like to hold a special family council. Set a specific time and special place in your home to meet.

If they ask you what this is all about, just tell them they'll find out that night, but not to worry. If someone has plans, ask them to please reschedule or get there after your meeting.

The idea here is to create an atmosphere of anticipation and high importance. You want your companion and children to be thinking all day about your upcoming gathering. If you prepare them this way, all eyes will be glued to you when you meet together.

If you are single and don't have a companion or children, see if you can meet in your home with one of your close friends, brother, sister, cousin, parent, or a clergy member—someone who cares about you and has always been there for you.

When you reach out to someone special in your life, you tap into a reservoir of ideas, inspiration, and motivation. There is a connection between all of us. You draw energy and light from special people in your life. These people are in your life for a reason.

But the final decision is ultimately yours. After all, it's your life.

When the meeting time arrives, shut off all TVs, cell phones, computers, radios, or other annoying gadgets.

Tell everyone that you're unhappy with the way your job hunt is going, but you're optimistic that something very positive is on the horizon. Share with them that you've decided to make a more concerted effort to find a job, and you need their help and support.

Go over your new routine with them. Explain to them that despite your best efforts, it could still be awhile before you find work, and it's even possible we *might* have to move.

If you get moans and groans about it, just tell everyone to relax. You said, *MAYBE*.

The reason you want to say this is because everyone needs time to process a big change. So, if you throw out the idea that you might have to move, it actually starts the change process.

Every action starts with a thought.

The more your family mulls this over in the coming weeks, the more accepting they will be if that day actually arrives. And your kids could react totally different than you expect. Kids adapt twice as fast as we do.

When I was fourteen years old, my father sat down with our family and announced that his company was thinking about relocating to Fort Lauderdale, Florida. He asked all of us how we felt about moving away.

We kids leapt for joy and did the Boogaloo around the living room slapping each other with high fives. We pictured ourselves hanging out on the beach, surfing, and plucking oranges off fruit trees in our front yard.

My folks were astonished that we didn't have a meltdown and threaten to move in with our friends until we graduated from high school.

We never did move, but we certainly were open to it if push came to shove.

Don't assume your kids will react negatively to a move. Ask them. Even if they're not in favor of it and give you a hard time about it, you are the parent and you have to do what you feel is in the best interest of your career and your family.

Chapter 4:
How to Make a Lasting First Impression in 30 Seconds

The great pleasure in life is doing what people say you cannot do.
~Walter Bagehot

Do you know the most popular job interview question of all time? This question will not only be on every list of job interview questions, but it is often the first question you will be asked.

Tell me about yourself.

The main purpose of this question is to get you talking.

Whoever is interviewing you wants to get an overall feel for you and your personality. They want to know how you express yourself and your choice of words, and observe your body language.

As you reply to this question, your interviewers are asking themselves:

- Are you confident?

- Are you open, straightforward, and interesting?

- Do you look them in the eye?

- What is important to you?

- Are you likable and enjoyable to be around?

Believe it or not, 60 percent of the decision to make you a job offer will be based on whether or not the interviewer likes you.

Fact: Managers hire people they like.

Studies have also concluded that the decision to hire you, or not, is made in the first five to ten minutes of the interview.

How can that be possible?

In that short period of time, you just hung up your coat and barely took your first sip of coffee. *Sheesh*, give me a chance!

So, your answer to this one question is pivotal in winning their approval, and ultimately receiving an offer.

Would you believe that your answer to this famous interview question **must be** no longer thirty to sixty seconds? Honestly! And I mean *no longer* than sixty seconds!

Fact: The main reason most candidates are rejected is because they communicate poorly. The second reason is they talk too much. A good interviewer can accurately judge your ability to communicate in less than a minute.

So, it is vitally important for you to create, and memorize, a thirty second commercial about yourself. This is sometimes affectionately referred to as your elevator speech.

Picture yourself walking into an elevator with someone you've never met before. From the time the elevator doors close until they open again on the tenth floor (about thirty seconds), you should be able to tell someone about yourself in a compelling way so as to leave them with a positive impression, and *wanting* to know more about you.

It can be done. It must be done. This is too important to do a half-baked job.

The best way to create your *Me in 30 Seconds* commercial is to set aside one to two hours of quiet time to reflect on your strengths, talents, interests, and values. It's ok if it takes you longer than this.

In a minute, I'll share with you seven steps to help you discover and internalize your strengths and character traits.

From the Heart: I'm sure that as you go through these seven areas of your life, there will be some pain or regret about something. Perhaps you didn't complete your college degree. You could be divorced, in a deteriorating relationship, or come from a dysfunctional family. You may have even had a brush with the law at some point in your life. Despite these issues, you still can find positives in each of these seven areas. Each of us is package of plusses and minuses. This exercise is all about discovering what is praiseworthy and good about you.

True story: Laura's self-esteem soars after learning about her ancestors

Laura was an avid genealogist. She loved researching and compiling her family history. She had traced her ancestors back to the early 1600s, still living here in America!

Laura was delighted to discover that among her descendants were patriots of the American Revolution, politicians, military leaders, and many others who left a noble legacy. She also discovered that the women in her line were devoted mothers and of tough pioneer stock, as she liked to say.

I asked her what had sparked her interest in family history, and why she is still so passionate about it after all these years.

Laura told me that she was raised in a dysfunctional home. Her father and grandfather were alcoholics. She only remembers seeing her paternal grandfather once in her entire life. Her paternal grandmother died before she was born.

Her father never participated in even one Christmas with the family.

Laura grew up in the "projects" of a major city and always felt inferior to others. Fortunately, she was blessed with a devoted mother who was her anchor and island of refuge in this troubled family.

Because of Laura's unhappy home life she always wondered if there were any good, honest people in her family line. As she started researching her family tree, she was amazed to discover that most of her ancestors were hard working, trustworthy, successful people.

Laura realized that her DNA was from this same noble stock. This was her history and legacy, too. Her self-esteem soared.

Checklist of 108 skills and character traits

Checklist of 108 Skills and Character Traits			
Ability work with others	Enterprising	Meticulous	Responsible
Accurate	Enthusiastic	Motivated	Results oriented
Ambitious	Entrepreneurial	Negotiation skills	Risk taker
Analytical	Fair minded	Open minded	Self sufficient
Business sense	Flexible	Optimistic	Sense of adventure
Caring nature	Forgiving	Organized	Sense of humor
Cheerful	Foresighted	Patient	Sense of urgency
Clear thinker	Friendly	Perceptive	Service oriented
Common sense	Generous	Persistent	Skillful
Communicate well	Global experience	Personal drive	Social
Concise	Global thinker	Persuasive	Stable
Confident	Goal oriented	Productive	Successful
Conscientious	Good judgment	Professional	Systematic
Cost-conscious	Grateful	Proficient	Tactful
Creative	Gratitude	Profit oriented	Take initiative
Decisive	Hard working	Progressive	Teachable
Dedicated	Helpful	Pioneering	Teacher
Dependable	Honest	Positive	Team builder
Detail oriented	Industrious	Practical	Tenacious
Determined	Innovative	Pragmatic	Thorough
Diligent	Insightful	Prepared	Tolerant
Diplomatic	Intuitive	Proactive	Trustworthy

Disciplined	Knowledgeable	Problem solver	Understanding
Driven	Leader	Quick learner	Versatile
Efficient	Learn quickly	Relationship builder	Visionary
Endurance	Logical	Resourceful	Willing
Energetic	Loyal	Respectful	Written skills

Check off ten to twelve skills/traits that best describe you.

Tip: This list is also available on my website at: http://www.job-interview-wisdom.com/good-interview-questions.html. Print a copy from my website and ask someone you know and trust to review the list. Ask them to check off which traits they believe apply to you. Compare your list with theirs. If you doubt your friend's assessment of one or two of these qualities, ask them for an example to convince you. Do the same in reverse. If they didn't check off a trait you believe you have, ask them why not.

I am...I have...I can

From your list of skills and traits, complete the following sentences:

- I am

- I have

- I can

Examples:

- I am a self-starter.

- I have analytical ability.

- I can give convincing sales presentations.

Practice saying these sentences out loud to develop a strong sense of ownership.

Off Track: It's not good enough to *just* write out your thoughts and feelings. You need to say them out loud. Verbalizing your strengths and character traits is good practice and builds your confidence. When you believe in yourself, it shows in your voice and body language.

Take a clean sheet of paper and fold it into 3 columns. Label the column headings:

- **Accomplishment 1**
- **Accomplishment 2**
- **Accomplishment 3**

Under each column heading, write the sub-heading: **skills and traits needed**.

Refer to your checklist of skills/traits and ask yourself the following question: How did I use one or more of these traits in past jobs or projects to solve a problem, make an improvement, or create something new? Try and come up with at least three accomplishments to write down.

> **Special Tip:** If you get stuck trying to come up with three accomplishments, ask yourself, "In what ways have I used this skill?" Let's say you checked off, cost-conscious, as one of your traits. Provide a work situation where you used this trait to save your company time or money.

Discovering your greatest strengths and character traits in 7 steps

Set aside one to two hours of quiet time where you can work without distractions or interruptions. This is a journey of self discovery. Enjoy this time with yourself.

1. Write down five positive words that describe you.

2. Write a short paragraph describing your family (can be your extended family).

3. List three of your hobbies or interests.

4. List three previous jobs, self-employment ventures, or school/ association projects.

5. List three of your accomplishments.

6. List your educational accomplishments.

7. List three of your values.

Don't worry about perfecting these seven steps just yet. The idea is to get you thinking about yourself in a positive, confident way. You're basically on deck in the batter's box swinging the bat and loosening up. We'll perfect these areas a little later.

Your strengths and character traits extend far beyond the boundaries of your job. Your qualities are attractive to prospective employers. Once you internalize these unique gifts, it will be easier to create a balanced, compelling thirty second statement about yourself.

Examples:

1. Write down five positive words that describe you.
   a. Honest
   b. Systematic
   c. Open minded
   d. Cost-conscious
   e. Disciplined

2. Write a short paragraph describing your family (can be your extended family).
   a. I enjoyed a happy childhood in the Midwest with my two brothers and one sister. My parents instilled within me a strong work ethic and expected me to earn money for my education and spending money. I've been happily married for ten years and enjoy spending time with my wife and three children. We spend time outdoors biking, hiking, and ice skating.

3. List three of your hobbies or interests.
   a. Aviation
   b. Photography
   c. Camping

4. List three of your previous jobs or self-employment projects.
   a. Engineering manager
   b. Engineering supervisor
   c. Manufacturing engineer

5. List your educational accomplishments
   a. BSME, Purdue University
   b. Spanish language skills

6. List three of your accomplishments.
   a. Private Pilot
   b. Military service - USMC
   c. Personal fitness

7. List three of your values.
   a. Honesty
   b. Integrity
   c. Perseverance

The above seven step exercise is for your eyes only. It is the blueprint for your *Me in 30 Seconds* statement. You'll refer to it as you develop your polished statement.

Pearl of Wisdom: Don't worry if you have a blemished past or you've made some bad choices that haunt you. Set those concerns aside for now. Despite our mistakes and shortcomings there is good in all of us. Everyone lives with regrets, but the road ahead is still wide open.

True story: I'm not that person anymore

My 20 year high school reunion was a lot of fun. I enjoyed seeing old school chums and laughing about some of the stunts we pulled as teenagers.

As the evening progressed, I glanced across the room and made eye contact with one of the class bullies. My heart sank as Steve starting walking towards me. As he approached, I vividly remembered several painful incidents from our high school years. I even felt a tinge of fear.

Here is how our conversation went:

Steve: Hi Mike! Remember me!?

Mike: (How could I forget?) Yeah, Steve…I remember you (somehow I forced a smile)

Steve: I bet you'd rather forget…wouldn't you?

Mike: Well…that was twenty years ago, Steve, and [*interrupted*]

Steve: I just want you to know…*I'm not that person anymore.*

Mike: OK…

Steve: I regret some of the things I said and did, and…*well*…I've changed. I'm sorry if I offended you, and just want to extend my hand of friendship. Hope we can move forward from here and let bygones be bygones.

Mike: (Gulp) OK…sure, Steve. I'm glad to hear that. (Shaking hands) Yes, of course. What is done is done. I'm so glad you came tonight. So, tell me...

I'll forever remember this moment from my twentieth high school reunion… and Steve's words:

I'm not that person anymore.

As I've met people over the years who continue to live with regrets, I've used Steve's words to help them move forward. This is also the perfect response to someone who still blames you for something you said or did in the past.

One of the great benefits of developing your thirty second elevator speech is restoring your self- image and self-confidence. Before you can convince others of your unique strengths and character traits, you have to convince yourself. Once you cross this threshold, you *can* literally make a positive first impression on people in just thirty seconds.

Tell me about yourself: 3 impressive example answers

Refer to the following examples to help you craft your own thirty-second elevator speech. Notice how each example includes four key elements:

- Something personal about you (adds warmth and depth)
- A very brief timeline sprinkled with strengths and values
- One notable accomplishment
- What you're looking for/Why you're here

Once you've perfected your thirty second elevator speech, memorize it, and practice it over and over again until it sounds natural and fluid.

Remember…companies aren't interested in your life story. They just want to get you talking to get a feel for your personality and communication skills. If you dazzle them in the first thirty seconds of your interview, it sets the stage for a positive interview.

Example 1: Me in 30 Seconds for a Manager

I grew up in Detroit and worked summers in high school to earn money for college. I'm a graduate of Michigan State and started my career with Ford as a marketing analyst.

I'm currently the sales manager for XYZ Corp, and have increased sales 10 percent a year for the past three years. I developed a great sales team, but the headwinds of the current recession have reduced market demand by at least 40 percent…and our regional office will be closed.

So, I was very excited to hear of your opening as I know I can improve your sales immediately.

In just thirty seconds, this candidate communicated the following ten strengths and qualities:

1. Grew up in a large metro area (can operate in fast-pace environment)
2. Paid for some of their college education
   a. Strong work ethic
   b. Not dependent on parents for everything
3. Graduated from a respected university
4. Started career with impressive major corporation with high hiring standards
5. Promoted to Sales Manager…must be pretty good (endorsement of others)
6. Good track record of increasing sales year over year (gets results)
7. Knows how to train and lead sales people to excel
8. Leaving job for something beyond his control
9. Excited about our company and opportunity (positive attitude)
10. Can make an immediate contribution to our success (exudes confidence)

Can you believe this candidate projected all of these strengths and qualities in just thirty seconds? Imagine all the non-verbal positives this candidate projected with their voice inflection, professional attire, grooming, eye contact, and confident manner.

Yeah, but isn't most of this stuff already on a candidate's resume?

Of course, but resumes can't talk. No one ever hired a resume.

Example 2: Me in 30 Seconds: (homemaker re-entering the job market)

For the past ten years I have been a dedicated homemaker. I graduated from Indiana University with a bachelor's degree in Business Administration.

I served in several volunteer organizations in recent years which allowed me to hone my skills in teaching, fund raising, recruiting new members, and planning large social events. I am a quick learner, not easily discouraged, and work well within small or large groups.

I'm very excited about rekindling my career, and will do whatever it takes to get the job done.

Example 3: Me in 30 Seconds: (hourly worker)

I grew up in a large family here in Nashville. I was expected to work hard and earn my own spending money.

I graduated from Nashville High School. During high school I always had a part time job, kept my grades up, and played four years on the varsity football team.

I have a good sense of humor. I am dependable, and can get along with just about anybody. I worked for Slave-Driver Corp as a Machinist for three years with a perfect attendance record. I would still be working there if the company hadn't gone under.

I am looking for long term employment with a solid local company, and will do whatever it takes to get the job done.

Chapter 5:
The Power of a Well Written Resume

*Strong people are made by opposition like
kites that go up against the wind.*
~Frank Harris

Now that you have your elevator speech down pat, we need to use it as a springboard to make sure your resume is doing you justice.

More than ever, companies today decide who they are going to interview, not only from the content of your resume, but its overall *look and feel*. It is one of the most important things you can do to improve your odds of landing an interview.

Most people let their egos take over and create a resume that basically screens them out. And by the way, it doesn't make any difference if your resume is done by a professional resume writer. Some of those resumes don't work very well either.

How do I know this?

Because for fifteen years I earned my daily bread by placing people with companies who gladly paid me a hefty fee to find candidates for them. I grew sick and tired of seeing outstanding professionals rejected all because someone at the company didn't like their resume.

So, I knew if I didn't fix this problem, I wouldn't eat…*simple as that*.

Special Tip: Your resume is a work in progress. It should be updated and tailored frequently. But the dos and don'ts of creating content and developing a good *Look and Feel* do not change.

Your resume is your personal advertisement of your skills, strengths, and accomplishments.

I can't emphasize this enough: Creating an attention grabbing resume is not easy. Expect to devote many hours writing and honing it to as near perfection as possible.

Trust me...*it's worth it!*

Companies rely on them more than ever to determine who gets interviewed and who gets rejected. You simply can't afford to do a half-baked job on your resume...*especially in this turbo-competitive job market.*

I've seen just about every outline of a resume you can imagine. It's a miracle I'm not permanently crossed-eyed and brain damaged by now. Believe me after you've looked at thousands of resumes, you know a good resume when you see one.

There are human resource specialists who spend half their day just reading, sorting, and screening resumes. Only a handful of resumes ever make it up the mountain to the hiring manager's desk. I don't know which job is worse, a resume reader or a tollbooth collector.

So, why am I telling you all this?

Fact: The number ONE complaint I hear from job seekers is that they get no response from a company after sending out a resume. *Nothing.* Just dead silence.

Reminds me of the old saying: *Treating someone with indifference is worse than bullying them.*

So how do you stop the silent treatment?

I will share with you a professional resume I consistently recommend to job seekers. It has a great look and feel, and it is easy for hiring authorities to read. Most candidates who use it experience more calls from companies inviting them to interview.

Does my resume work all of the time?

Of course not. Nothing works 100 percent of the time. But it *will* improve your batting average, and in some cases, remarkably so.

Special Tip for Long-Term Unemployed: When you've been unemployed for six months or longer, desperation sets in. Many frustrated job seekers add more and more information to their resume in an attempt to make something happen. Resist doing this. *Less is more* when it comes to creating a powerful resume. The more information you add to your resume, the more reasons you give prospective employers to screen you out. Keep your resume simple so it draws people in and leaves them hungry for more. See your resume as an invitation to meet you.

In the next section, I'll take you step by step through each section of my resume. I explain the logic of each section, words and phrases you might want to use, best formats, the length of your resume, other dos and don'ts, and common resume mistakes to avoid.

I've also created this same resume with my notes written in each section explaining why you should build your resume this way.

Lots of books and websites have been written about other resume outlines, such as functional resumes, but that is beyond the scope this book. For now, I just want to share with you one resume format that has been very successful for many of my candidates.

Best outline of an attention-grabbing resume

John Doe

123 Drewry Lane
Anytown, USA

Home: 219-555-1234   E-Mail: jdoe@aol.com

OBJECTIVE

Sales Account Manager

ACCOMPLISHMENTS

- 7+ years of sales experience in a fast paced manufacturing environment
- Exceeded sales targets by at least 10% for past 3 years
- Trained and mentored 15 new inside sales representatives
- Launched 23 new products
- Developed successful sales strategies resulting in 2 new markets
- Member of company task force for product improvements

EMPLOYMENT

ABC Corp, Chicago, IL   2000 - Present
$110 million division of Mega Corp, headquartered in Chicago, IL. ABC Corp manufactures high-pressure industrial and mobile hydraulic components.

Senior Account Manager

Responsible for new business development, marketing, technical sales presentations, and client relations. Manage one of the largest branch territories in North America. Supervise, motivate, and train 2 inside sales representatives in products and effective client servicing. Implement effective sales and marketing strategies. Plan and conduct seminars for new product features and benefits.

- Top producing account manager in Chicago for 3 consecutive years
- Achieved 100% customer retention in a struggling open territory
- Ranked in top 10% of producers for NA sales volume for 3 straight years
- One of 6 associates selected to participate in a company-wide product and procedural improvement task force; video was distributed to all associates which streamlined improvement process
- Detroit, MI - worked closely with upper management to identify market potential, and assist in developing a sales action plan

(John Doe page two)

XYZ Corporation, Chicago, IL   1987-2000
$200 million manufacturer of machinings and stampings for the Automotive Industry

Account Manager   1991-2000

Responsible for all sales presentations, marketing programs, and support materials for the sale of commercial and electronic printing. Extensive cold calling, market penetration, and tracking of accounts. Created specialized marketing plans and sales proposals for key accounts.

- Expanded client base from 100 to 300 over 9 years with 95% retention
- Increased sales every year by at least 10%
- Developed marketing material to support our sales process

Customer Service Representative   1987-1991

Involved in customer service and communications for sales support. Gained an excellent background in company procedures, printing processes, and the sales cycle. Promoted and organized various sales and marketing projects.

QRS Stock Brokers, Schaumburg, IL   1987

Summer internship

Compiled daily reports for traders and brokers. Planned and conducted a stock valuation and analysis research project to gain experience of stock market operations and investing.

EDUCATION

University of Notre Dame, South Bend, IN
BSME, graduated Cum Laude.

SKILLS

Proficient in MS Office, Lotus 123, and PowerPoint

Best outline of an attention-grabbing resume with commentary

John Doe

123 Drewry Lane
Anytown, USA

Home: 219-555-1234   E-Mail: jdoe@aol.com

OBJECTIVE [Bold headings act like a table of contents and make scanning and navigating your resume easier]

Sales Account Manager [Tell the company what job you are applying for or what position you are targeting. Don't go overboard with a lot of meaningless fluff words. The more specific you are the better a company can match you. Avoid being too broad thinking the company will find a spot for you somewhere. It's OK to list 2 or 3 related positions here, especially if you are willing to step down from a management role.]

ACCOMPLISHMENTS [Hit them right between the eyes with 5-6 eye-popping accomplishments to quickly grab their attention. Be careful not to go wild and fill up half a page. It's important you provide specific measurable results. Write actual numerals 7 or 8, instead of seven or eight. Notice how these numbers jump right out at you. Your eyes are naturally drawn to the numbers.]

- 7+ years of sales experience in a fast paced manufacturing environment.
- Exceeded sales targets by at least 10% for past 3 years
- Trained and mentored 15 new Inside sales representatives
- Launched 23 new products
- Developed successful sales strategies resulting in 2 new markets
- Member of company task force for product improvements

EMPLOYMENT

ABC Corp, Chicago, IL   2000 - Present
$110 million division of Mega Corp, headquartered in Chicago, IL. ABC Corp manufactures high-pressure industrial and mobile hydraulic components. [Write 1-2 very short sentences in italics under the company name providing the following minimal information: their annual sales and what is their main product or service. This is so important! There are a lot of companies out there no one has ever heard of before. Make it easy for a prospective employer to get a feel for the size and scope of a company you've worked for without having to Google it.]

Senior Account Manager [It may be better to use a generic, more descriptive job title instead of your official title. Some companies--especially foreign companies--have really cute job titles that only people in their culture understand. You might be a Customer Satisfaction Program Manager, but no one outside your company has a clue what you do. Everyone else calls your job a Quality Manager. So, write that down. The idea here is to communicate as clearly as possible what you do. Make it easy for them. This is in no way unethical or dishonest.]

Responsible for new business development, marketing, technical sales presentations, and client relations. Manage one of the largest branch territories in North America. Supervise, motivate, and train 2 inside sales representatives in products and effective client servicing. Implement effective sales and marketing strategies. Plan and conduct seminars for new product features and benefits. [This section is basically a 3 to 4 short sentence job description. Keep it very short. You're just trying to share with someone 3-4 of your key job responsibilities. You can tell them about the rest of your duties in the interview.]

- Top producing account manager in Chicago for 3 consecutive years
- Achieved 100% customer retention in a struggling open territory
- Ranked in top 10% of producers for NA sales volume for 3 straight years
- One of 6 associates selected to participate in a company-wide product and procedural improvement task force; video was distributed to all associates which streamlined improvement process.
- Detroit, MI - worked closely with upper management to identify market potential, and assist in developing a sales action plan. [List 4-5 accomplishments. Remember to show measureable results. Type actual numbers 7 or 8, not seven or eight. As a general rule, list more accomplishments with your most recent experience. Your prior company should show 3-4 accomplishments and so on. After you go back 12-15 years you might have only one accomplishment or none. If you've only been at your current company for a year, but you were at your prior company 8 years, then it's ok to reverse this. It is what it is.]

John Doe page two [Make sure to put your name on the 2nd page of your resume. It's also a good idea to put page numbers in the footer. I always liked, x of y pages. Again, make it easy for people.]

XYZ Corporation, Chicago, IL   1987-2000
$200 million manufacturer of machinings and stampings for the Automotive Industry.

Account Manager   1991-2000

Responsible for all sales presentations, marketing programs, and support materials for the sale of commercial and electronic printing. Extensive cold calling, market penetration, and tracking of accounts. Created specialized marketing plans and sales proposals for key accounts.

- Expanded client base from 100 to 300 over 9 years with 95% retention
- Increased sales every year by at least 10%
- Developed marketing material to support our sales process [Notice how the number of accomplishments is fewer the farther back in time we go. It's still important, but this happened 10-15 years ago when we were still using Windows 95.]

Customer Service Representative   1987-1991

Involved in customer service and communications for sales suppor. Gained an excellent background in company procedures, printing processes, and the sales cycle. Promoted and organized various sales and marketing projects.

QRS Stock Brokers, Schaumburg, IL. 1987 [Notice how there are no accomplishments listed here since you worked there 23 years ago and it's not that relevant today. You only need to show 20 years of job history. This is a good way to prevent age discrimination. Ignore this if you are an executive. Believe it or not, some 70+ year old executives are being recruited out of retirement to turn around troubled companies on the brink of disaster.]

Summer internship

Compiled daily reports for traders and brokers. Planned and conducted a stock valuation and analysis research project to gain experience of stock market operations and investing.

EDUCATION

University of Notre Dame, South Bend, IN
BSME, graduated Cum Laude [Don't put the date you graduated unless you are between the ages of 22-35. Candidates in this age bracket are highly sought after, so you want to broadcast to the world that you are young. Older workers want to definitely leave off their graduation date. Don't give a company any information to prejudge you.]

SKILLS [Certifications and training can be listed here as well, but don't go overboard. Other resume no-no's: Don't list your hobbies or

outside activities. Don't type on your resume, references available upon request. Everyone already knows this, so it just wastes space on your resume.]
Proficient in MS Office, Lotus 123, and PowerPoint.

7 simple resume dos and don'ts

Let's build your resume step by step and go over the logic behind it. Before we do, I want you to think about why my resume sample is so well received by companies.

I'll give you a hint.

Hiring authorities don't have to do any research to figure out what products or services your prior companies produce. Make it easy for people to know this by simply reading your resume.

FACT: The only purpose of a resume is to win a face-to-face interview with a hiring authority.

The secret to a good resume is to provide just enough information about you, in an *easy-to-read-and-understand-format,* to leave a positive impression and develop curiosity to know more. Think about how newspaper headlines draw you in and the first few sentences of the article peak your interest. So you continue reading. The same strategy works with your resume.

Check your ego at the door when you're writing your resume. If you provide too much information you run the risk of getting screened out. Save the best of you for your interview.

General recommendations for my resume writing example:

1. Use Arial or Calibri 10 or 12-pt font. Always use the color black throughout. Never use red or other colors.

   Comments: Arial is a simple, clean font that is easy to read. If your job history is short, use 11 or 12-pt type. The first time someone lays their eyes on your resume, they are not going to read every word of it. They're going to scan it to see how it's formatted and to see if any key job requirement words or phrases jump out at them.

You want the *look and feel* of your resume to invite the reader to want to know more about you. In ten seconds or less, they are going to decide whether or not your resume is worth their valuable time to actually read.

2. Create your resume in a Word (.doc) or PDF format. Avoid templates and borders.

    Comments: Most companies can easily store these universal formats in their resume database. They are easy to attach and forward to others in the company. Funky templates and borders often fall apart when emailed and can mess up your content.

    If you have the most current version of MS Word, use the "save as" feature to save it in a Word 97-2003 format. Why? This is a standard doc format that is compatible with most database systems. If a company hasn't upgraded their version of Word to the latest version, they may not be able to open your attachment. They won't email you back to tell you either. So, you'll be out of luck and won't even know it. To avoid all of this, just provide your resume in a PDF format as it is compatible with all systems and versions.

3. Always include your full address and contact information.

    Comments: For some reason, some folks are leaving off their address these days. Their contact information consists of their name, email address, and cell phone number. This is a bad idea for several reasons.

    When you do this, you are shouting: *"I don't trust you."* Second, companies and recruiters store your resume in sophisticated databases that allow them to search by location, area code, and other factors. They may never be able to find you again in their database.

    Third, companies and recruiters don't like it when you do this. Do you want hiring authorities to be annoyed the second they lay their eyes on your resume?

One reason folks leave their address off their resume is because they don't want to be eliminated as a serious candidate for a relocation issue. You may live in California, but want desperately to move back home to Ohio. Many times a company will see the California address and read no further because they don't want to pay for a major relocation.

What the company doesn't realize is the candidate is renting and is more than willing to relocate at their own expense. So, the candidate tries to minimize this risk by leaving off their physical address.

Tip: If you are willing to pay your own relocation expenses to move back to your home town, just put a family member's address on your resume. Your area code doesn't matter anymore as people often carry over their cell phone numbers no matter where they live. Companies will see the local address and won't automatically eliminate you because of potential relocation costs.

---

4. Minimize using special effects like **bold**, *italics*, and underlining. If overdone, it makes your resume look amateurish.

5. You don't need to limit your resume to one page. Honestly!

   Comments: The one page resume rule is a myth. I have no idea how this ever got started. It probably originated in colleges because most students barely have enough information to fill up one page.

   It is perfectly OK to have a two to three page resume, but no longer than three pages. Obviously, if you're mid-to-late career, you can't possibly fit your experience and accomplishments on one page. If you're late in your career, one way to keep your resume from being five pages long is to just outline your experience for the past twenty years. Beyond twenty years, how relevant is that experience anyway?

Many companies age discriminate, although they all would jump up and down in denial if they heard me make this statement. Only sharing your past twenty years of experience is a perfectly good way to conceal your age without being dishonest or deceptive.

6. Read your resume out loud. This forces you to actually read every single word on your resume to see how it sounds. This will also help you spot errors and poorly worded phrasing.

7. *Last but not least...*check, double check, and triple check for spelling errors! You might be able to get away with one typo, but two typos and your resume will probably be rejected. Three errors...*forget it.* Even automated spell checkers miss words like there/their, its/it's, compound words, and other wording specific to your industry.

Special Tip: If your resume is well received, you may be directed to fill out the company's online application. Most of these are time consuming and a pain to fill out. Even after you spend time carefully filling one out, you still may never hear from the company again. To expedite filling out these buggers, first create most of information they usually ask for in Microsoft Notepad. The reason you want to use Notepad is because it is in Text format. This is the format most compatible with web-based documents and forms. This way you can Copy and Paste your information from Notepad into the application. It makes it go much faster, you won't make typos, and you won't have to work hard at wording statements. Also, you avoid getting timed out on the company website, forcing you to start all over again.

Chapter 6:
Fourteen Potent Truths and Myths about Popular Job Search Methods

If a man could have half his wishes,
he would double his troubles.
~Benjamin Franklin

We live in a world of sound bytes and quick fixes. Everywhere you turn there is a website, book, article, or advertisement touting simple solutions to complex problems.

Think about all the hype surrounding dieting, fitness, investing, cosmetic surgery, match-making, and getting out of debt. Job search advice is no exception. Unfortunately, there are a lot of myths, misconceptions, and flat out bad advice about job hunting and career changing.

When you are trying with all of your might to find a job, and nothing happens, you feel it's your fault and there must be something terribly wrong with you. This attitude, left unchecked, not only leads to discouragement and downright depression, but also a feeling of hopelessness about just how you are ever going to find a job.

Pearl of Wisdom: How we *think* influences how we *feel*. How we *feel* moves us to take *action*—constructively or destructively. Taking no action is still an action. When we are hopeful and confident, the tailwind of momentum kicks in and helps push us forward.

When you know why one job search approach works well, and why another falls short, you become more hopeful, confident, and motivated. You start creating your own luck.

To prove my point, I'm going to ask you to take a short quiz to see just how much you know about the job hunting arena. Yes...right now. This will be a real eye-opener for you.

	Short Quiz to Test Your Job Search Savvy		
	Questions	True	False
1	Responding to want ads on Monster, CareerBuilder, and HotJobs is one of the best ways to find a job.		
2	Mass mailing your resume to hundreds of employers or recruiters is an effective way to find a job quickly.		
3	Telephoning a list of employers, without knowing if they have a job opening, is a waste of time and annoying to employers.		
4	Employers only use temp agencies for part time, minimum wage type positions.		
5	Physically walking into every temp agency/staffing firm in town with your resume in hand is a good way to find a job.		
6	Twitter, Facebook, and LinkedIn are social websites with little value to job seekers.		
7	Employers prefer to promote someone from within, hire a part-time employee, or hire a temp/contract worker.		
8	Employers prefer to hire people who have been referred to them by one of their employees.		
9	Employers often use executive search firms to help them fill key leadership positions.		
10	Posting your resume on the Internet is one of the best ways to get found by employers—especially if you are unemployed.		
11	In today's economy, it's a "buyer's market" and employers have plenty of good candidates to choose from.		
12	You sent your resume to a company in response to their want ad. They haven't contacted you in a week. If you follow up with a phone call to the hiring manager you risk upsetting them and not being considered for the position.		
13	Expect above average results when you target specific companies and apply for jobs posted on their websites.		
14	The Jet Stream of most job opportunities is with small to medium size companies.		

Answers to the job search quiz, and best strategies to win interviews

1. **Responding to want ads on Monster, CareerBuilder, and HotJobs is one of the best ways to find a job.**

FALSE

FACTS:

- Only a 3.6 percent success rate, depending on your occupation; IT, engineering, and technical jobs fair better at 10 to 12 percent.
- Big job boards are rapidly losing ground to social networking sites, like newspaper want-ads did to the Internet in early 2000.
- On average, companies receive 300 to 600 resumes per job post.
- Getting an interview via the big job boards is like getting picked to audition for American Idol.

YOUR BEST STRATEGY:

- Spend the least amount of your job search time on the major boards, 30 minutes a day at the most.
- Instead of going out to each major job board, use Indeed.com. It aggregates jobs from numerous job sites and brings them to you.
- Anticipate few, if any, responses when you apply. This is normal for everyone. So, don't take it personally and get all depressed. It's not you.
- Don't keep applying to the same Monster job if it is posted multiple times. This could actually screen you out. No reply means, no thanks.
- Don't apply to a job you are not qualified for hoping either you will get lucky or they will offer you another job. This annoys employers and recruiters.

2. **Mass mailing your resume to hundreds of employers or recruiters is an effective way to find a job quickly.**

FALSE

FACTS:

- Only a 7 percent success rate at best. Other studies show even worst results, one out of a thousand.
- Most executives and managers receive an unmanageable number of resumes a day. They simply can't read them all.
- Emailing or snail mailing your unsolicited resume is considered junk mail. What do you do with junk mail?

YOUR BEST STRATEGY:

- Simply do not mass email your resume. This also protects you from becoming overexposed.
- Never, EVER use a resume blaster service to shotgun your resume to thousands of companies and recruiters.
- Selectively share your resume only though a trusted source. You need to control who sees your resume and when.
- Make sure you are on LinkedIn and your profile is well written with key words about your skills. Don't forget to include your professional photo. Eighty percent of executive recruiters use LinkedIn to find candidates. Approximately 70 percent of major corporations also use LinkedIn.

---

3. **Telephoning a list of employers, without knowing if they have a job opening, is a waste of time and annoying to employers.**

FALSE

FACTS:

- This is one of the best ways to find a job because very few people do it. Most job seekers use the Internet because it's easier.
- Eighty percent of all available jobs are not advertised, so they are invisible to the public.

- Companies prefer to find people through employee referrals instead of hiring from the general public.
- A manager may be thinking about replacing someone, but can't advertise this. So, your timing is good when you call in.

YOUR BEST STRATEGY:

- Go to your local public library and get a library card. Use it to get on library website to access company directories.
- A good online company database is ReferenceUSA. It contains names of managers and company phone numbers. Most libraries allow online access.
- Compile a list of twenty-five to thirty companies a day and simply call them. In chapter nine I'll share with you an effective cold calling script.
- Spend most of your job hunting time calling hiring managers, not Human Resources. You are less likely to get thrown into "the system".
- The more time you spend *talking* to a hiring manager instead of relying on email, the greater your chances of getting a job offer.

---

4. **Employers only use temp agencies/staffing firms for part time, minimum wage type positions.**

FALSE

FACTS:

- Temp agencies and staffing firms now hire across most job levels, including managers and executives.
- To see the varied job categories for temp workers, go to: http://www.net-temps.com/. This is a very good job board for temp/contract opportunities.

YOUR BEST STRATEGY:

- Contact every temp agency/staffing firm in your home town. Many local companies regularly give them jobs to fill.
- Don't be afraid to take a temp job. You can quit at any time. It pays the bills and they could hire you full time.
- An offer for a temp job is like being asked out on a date. An offer for a perm job is like a marriage proposal.

---

5. **Physically walking into every temp agency/staffing firm in town with your resume is a good way to find a job.**

TRUE

FACTS:

- Temp/contract hiring always leads out of a recession.
- Seventy-five percent of all US companies utilize contract workers in one fashion or another. This has been steadily increasing for several years.
- In August 2010, perm jobs fell by 54,000 jobs, but temp jobs increased by 17,000.
- Unlike executive search firms, temp agencies/staffing firms need an inventory of candidates to send out to their client companies.
- The hiring process for a temp job is twice as fast as for a perm job.
- Many temp/staffing firms offer health insurance, vacation, retirement plans, and other benefits.

YOUR BEST STRATEGY:

- Map out every temp agency/staffing firm in your community, dress for a job interview, and physically walk in their door with your resume in hand prepared for a face-to-face job interview. It's important you leave them with a positive first impression.

- Every Friday, call the temp/staffing firms you visited and let them know you are still available.
- Don't just work with one temp agency/staffing firm. Work with as many as you can. They all have different client companies.

---

6. **Twitter, Facebook, and Linked In are social websites with little value to job seekers.**

FALSE

FACTS:

- There are more than 100 million Twitter users, and growing by leaps and bounds.
- Companies and recruiters report finding higher quality candidates through social networking sites.
- In a recent survey, 80 percent of companies plan to use social networks to find or attract candidates.
- Twenty-four percent of candidates disclose their social networking presence when applying for a job. This tells companies you are in step with the times and will likely bring fresh ideas to the company.
- Companies are cutting back on want ads because social networking is free and delivers better candidates.

YOUR BEST STRATEGY:

- If you're a professional, you simply *must have* a well written professional profile on LinkedIn; being on Facebook and Twitter is a plus, but not as imperative.
- Social networking should be part of your long term career strategy, even if you love your new job. There is no such thing today as job security.
- If you don't participate in social networking, you'll be seen by hiring authorities as old school and out of step with the times.

- Make sure you have an attractive, professional photo of yourself on these sites.
- Learn all you can about personal branding to develop your own powerful personal profile.
- Do not post rude, crude, or silly posts. Anything you post should add value and be useful to others.
- Take the time to study and learn the best job search strategies for each social networking site.
- Do not rely solely on these sites to find a job. It's one of the best networking tools, but not the only tool. Picking up the phone and talking to people still works.

---

7. **Employers prefer to promote someone from within, hire a part-time employee, or hire a temp/contract worker.**

TRUE

FACTS:

- This is a low-risk risk strategy for employers because they know you, trust you, and have experienced your work.
- Internal transfers and promotions accounted for 39 percent of all hires in 2008 versus 28 percent in 2007.
- The recession of 2009-10 is making it more difficult today for companies to draw from their bench due to leaner organizations.
- Temp-to-hire positions always lead out of a recession and are a low risk way for employers to hire quickly. They also get to try before they buy, but so do you.

YOUR BEST STRATEGY:

- If you are unemployed, try and get hired as a temp, contract worker, consultant, or part time employee.

- See previous comments in item 5, on the best ways to approach temp/staffing firms.

---

8. Employers prefer to hire people who have been referred to them by one of their employees.

TRUE

FACTS:

- Recent survey of corporations revealed that 27 percent of their hiring comes through referrals, one in four.
- Getting referred into a company by an insider is by far the best way to get a job.
- Seventy percent of the most effective job search strategies involve networking, leaving 30 percent for all the other ways.
- This saves companies time and eliminates the pain of having to sift through resumes and interview lots of people

YOUR BEST STRATEGY:

- Spend the majority of your job search efforts networking with people on the phone, in a group, and through social networking sites.
- Park your ego. Ask people for their help and influence. Most people want to help you, but they aren't mind readers.
- Develop a long term networking strategy. This way the next time you need a job, you will have tons of connections—much more on this in a later chapter.
- Make sure you give back and help others when you're back in the saddle. What goes around comes around.

---

9. **Employers often use executive search firms to help them fill key leadership positions.**

TRUE

FACTS:

- Working with a search firm is a low yield strategy for non-professional, rank-and-file type positions, less than 3 percent success rate.
- Some employers always use an executive recruiter for executive level positions: CEO, CFO, CIO, VP, president, director, division level managers.
- Some may not have the time or personnel to do a search on their own.
- Some may want to replace someone and must keep the search confidential.
- If a company is experiencing rapid growth, strong sales, or even struggling with problems, they sometimes prefer to pay someone else to go through the lengthy process of finding, interviewing, and screening candidates.
- If a company is in a remote location, or a location with a poor reputation, they may need a recruiting firm to help attract candidates.
- If a company has a long standing relationship with an executive recruiter, they trust their referrals much like they would one of their employees.

YOUR BEST STRATEGY:

- Refer to the book *The Kennedy Directory of Executive Recruiters*. You can look up e-mails and phone numbers of executive recruiters by their industry and job specialties. Only approach recruiters who specialize in your job specialty; otherwise, it's like you going to an orthopedic surgeon for a root canal.

- Never email blast or shotgun your resume to recruiting firms.
- If contacted by an executive recruiter, always try to be helpful and courteous.
- Don't refer to executive recruiters as headhunters. Most recruiters don't like it.

---

10. **Posting your resume on the Internet is one of the best ways to get found by employers, especially if you are unemployed.**

FALSE

FACTS:

- Employers prefer you come to them via their website, an online ad, or through an employee referral.
- Employers have enough resumes to read without having to go out on the Internet and dig through millions more.
- You run the risk of your current employer finding your resume online and giving you the boot.
- Many top-notch executive recruiters won't work with you if your resume is posted on any of the major job boards because they consider you overexposed.

YOUR BEST STRATEGY:

- **Must Do:** Create an in-depth, professional profile on LinkedIn. Anyone who is anybody is using this powerful free resource. Most companies today will search for you LinkedIn profile if they like your resume.
- You can also create a fan page on Facebook that is separate from your personal Facebook. Your fan page can be public whereas your personal page can be just for close friends and family.

---

11. **In today's economy, it's a "buyer's market" and employers have plenty of good candidates to choose from.**

FALSE

FACTS:

- Employers want to hire people who excel at what they do and are in the top 20 percent of the workforce. Most of these folks are employed and in short supply.
- The vast majority of the resumes companies get are from folks who are average or below average in skills, attitude, and promote-ability.
- "A-Player" candidates are *always* in demand, especially in engineering or high technology type positions.

YOUR BEST STRATEGY:

- If you excel at what you do, a weak economy will not be insurmountable. Follow the best job search strategies (networking) and you will break through.
- Consistent daily effort is required and results *will* follow. If this hasn't been the case for you, keep reading this book.
- Stop listening to the negative macro trends about the overall economy. It will only de-motivate you and slow down your job search.

---

12. **You sent your resume to a company in response to their want ad. They haven't contacted you in a week. If you follow up with a phone call to the hiring manager you risk upsetting them and not being considered for the position.**

FALSE

FACTS:

- Very few people call the manager to follow up on their resume because they're either chicken or too lazy.

- This makes you stand out from other candidates. Managers will often pull up your resume or let you email another one to them.
- Human Resources may have screened you out and the hiring manager never saw your resume. You now have a second chance.
- What do you have to lose by calling the hiring manager? Connecting with a hiring manager is always a good thing.
- When I was a hiring manager, I hired people who called me. In some cases, I was simply overwhelmed with resumes.

YOUR BEST STRATEGY:

- Call the hiring manager the week after you've applied for a position.
- Best place to find the name of the hiring manager is on LinkedIn.
- If you can't find the name of the manager, call into the switchboard and ask to be connected. Eighty percent of the time they will connect you, especially if you use my script in chapter nine.
- Yes...leave a voice mail. Let technology work for you. He/she will likely look up your resume before they call you back.
- If you don't get a call back, call again a week later, then move on. Don't become a stalker candidate and keep calling. No call back means "no thanks".

---

13. Expect above average results when you target specific companies and apply for jobs posted on their websites.

TRUE

FACTS:

- One in five hires, or 20.7 percent of company new hires come through their website.
- Eighty percent of the time, jobs posted to company websites are not advertised on Monster or other big boards.

- Jobs posted to company websites are also designed to attract internal candidates.
- Some companies post bogus jobs just to harvest resumes for future "tough to fill" jobs or job requisitions they hope to get approved in the next two to three months.
- Some companies will post jobs on Twitter before posting them anywhere else. They do this because job postings are free, but more importantly; "people in step with the times" are out on Twitter.

YOUR BEST STRATEGY:

- Research the emerging companies in your industry and follow them.
- Go to your local library for access to free on-line directories of corporations searchable by SIC codes, products, size, and locations.
- Many major corporations provide search agents on their website that will email you when they post a new job in your specialty.
- Use Twitter to follow the buzz on companies of high interest to you.
- *Never* just apply to a job on a company website without first exhausting your efforts to find someone on the inside who can refer you to the hiring authority—more on how to do this in chapter seven. You'll be amazed at how connected you are and who some of the movers/shakers your connections know.

---

14. The Jet Stream of most job opportunities is with small to medium size companies.

TRUE

FACTS:

- Half of all the jobs in the USA are in companies with fewer than 500 employees.
- **Small company:** $150M in sales or less; fewer than 500 employees; mostly privately held.

- **Medium company:** $150 - 750M in sales; between 500 and 2,500 employees; privately and publicly held.
- **Large company:** $750M or more in sales; over 2,500 employees; mostly publicly held.
- Two out of three job openings are with small to medium companies.

YOUR BEST STRATEGY:

- Research company websites to get a feel for the size of an organization.
- Look up a company on LinkedIn to see if there is any information posted. Then, try to connect with an employee through your LinkedIn connections.
- Go to your local library for access to free on-line directories of corporations searchable by SIC codes, products, size, and locations.

Anything surprise you as you worked through this little exercise?

Pearl of Wisdom: Many times our *perception* of reality is not *true* reality. How do you *know* something is really true? Too often we accept hyperbole as fact—like Monster Board is the fastest way to find a job—or we stubbornly hang onto our beliefs and opinions until a painful event comes along that alters our point of view, like a long stretch of unemployment. In many cases, the frustrations we endure are due to incomplete or inaccurate knowledge about something or someone. Once this is corrected, our attitude, motivation, and *results* can improve *immediately*.

Chapter 7:
Social Networking: The New Way Companies Look for Job Candidates

There are no shortcuts to any place worth going.
~Beverly Sills

What exactly is social networking?

Many people have heard about it, but aren't exactly sure what it is, or how it will benefit them. Others think they understand it, but go about it poorly because they are lacking in social networking etiquette and protocol.

Still others think it's stupid and won't even give it a chance.

Will it help you find a job?

Yes, if you go about it the right way, and don't get carried away with all the hype.

Is it difficult or uncomfortable to do?

There is a learning curve to it—like any new skill—but if you take the time to learn it properly, it is well worth it. And it can even be fun and almost addictive.

So, what's the big deal? Why should you even bother with it?

Have you ever heard the old saying: *It's not what you know, but whom you know?*

You might chuckle at this saying as you slowly shake your head from side to side, but it's really true. Do you know someone who received a promotion or landed a job simply because they knew someone with the power to pull a few strings?

Sure you do. We all do.

Social networking levels the playing field for you. It is a tool to introduce you to influential people with the power to help you solve one or more of your problems. That includes the problem of unemployment, under-employment, or a career going nowhere.

FACT: Seventy percent of the most effective job search strategies are through networking.

In a nutshell, social networking is a powerful way to expand your network of trusted relationships, many of whom will be delighted to hear from you and eager to help you.

Honestly!

Keeping it Simple: A brief history of how companies find people for their job openings:

- 1985-1995:   Newspaper ads
- 1995-2005:   Internet ads
- 2005- 2015:   Social networking

The top 3 social networking sites today, in order of importance, are:

1. LinkedIn
2. Facebook
3. Twitter

Even if you think you are an expert on one of more of these sites, take the time to carefully read the chapters to follow as I will share with you important insights on how to use these sites effectively to your career advantage.

Most people only tap into 30 percent, or less, of the wealth these sites offer. Each site is different and offers unique ways to connect and stay in touch with people. The best news is all of these sites are free to use and can provide you with incredible career leverage.

It is beyond the scope of this book to provide you with detailed instructions on how to set up an account and perform all the various functions of each social networking site. My goal is to share with you what is unique about each one, why they work so well, and what you need to do to get in the game. I will then point you to other credible resources—that I have carefully researched—that will instruct you on how to navigate each site and use their many features to your maximum benefit.

Keep in mind, there is a learning curve to social networking. It will take you a few weeks to grasp it fully. But you simply *must* take the time to learn it. You will not be disappointed.

Proceed slowly and only focus on one social networking site at a time. Once you get the hang of one site, move on to the next one. It takes most people six to eight weeks of learning and actual hands on experience to become fairly proficient. This seems like a long time, but it will be well worth it, and actually quite fun.

Special Tip: Look at developing your social networking skills like a major project. In the beginning of your training, block out one to two hours a day to focus on it. As the days go by, it will soon become second nature to you like any new skill.

Social networking doesn't end when you find a job. Even if you love your new job and plan to stay put until you retire, you always want to maintain your network of connections. We live in a day and age when you never know if your company will be closed, sold, downsized, or merged.

You could be happy as a lark one day, and the next day find yourself walking out to your car carrying a box full of your office stuff.

Your social network is your lifeline and insurance against unforeseen career-wrecking events.

LinkedIn: Your online professional profile

LinkedIn started out in the living room of co-founder Reid Hoffman in the fall of 2002. It officially opened on May 5, 2003 (affectionately referred to by employees as Cinco de LinkedIn). By year's end, they employed fourteen people and had forty-five hundred subscribers.

Today (2010), LinkedIn has over eighty million subscribers in over two hundred countries. A new member joins LinkedIn approximately every second. Half of their members are outside the US.

What is unique about LinkedIn and why should you care?

Let me put it to you this way. What would be your reaction if I approached you and said: *"I have this really cool networking system that I want to share with you that will..."*

1. allow you to easily find and stay in touch with current and past co-workers, bosses, suppliers, customers, friends, and other business partners who you value and trust;

2. provide you with automatic email updates whenever your connections change jobs, receive a promotion, relocate, change their phone number or email address, or change their LI profile;

3. allow you to discover the connections of your contacts for deeper networking;

4. provide you with your own personal web page outlining your professional credentials, accomplishments, associations, and business connections visible to only those you approve, with the option to share some or all of this information with the public;

5. allow others to contact you via secure private email about career opportunities, new ventures, expertise requests, reference requests, consulting offers, job inquiries, business deals, or simply to touch base (you decide which of these you want to receive, or block);

6. allow former bosses, customers, suppliers, friends, or suppliers to write a glowing testimonial about your professional accomplishments or leadership abilities on your personal profile page (you approve and edit these testimonials before they are published on your site);

7. provide you with a brief overview of thousands of public corporations, and who in your network—*or your connections' network*—work there;

8. allow you to view job postings from thousands of companies then, with a simple click of your mouse, you can see if anyone in your network works there or has a friend who works there who can personally put your resume in front of the right hiring authority instead of going through "the system" and risk getting lost in the piles of resumes companies receive on a daily basis;

9. allow you to join, for free, several LinkedIn groups with access to every member (groups include: college alumni, corporate groups, professional groups, non-profit groups, and many other associations; you can even create your own group); and,

10. allows you to interact with other professionals in a forum setting to debate industry problems and issues—often times visited by hiring authorities who participate and could be impressed with your input.

Have I got your attention yet?

Would you believe you get all of this for free? Would you believe that once you're set up on LinkedIn and know how to navigate around the site, all of the above activity could be done in fifteen to twenty minutes a day?

Seriously!

What is even more unbelievable is that LinkedIn gets most of their traffic Monday through Friday, during normal business hours, not on the weekend as you might suspect.

This means most people do their LinkedIn networking at work.

If you still aren't convinced that LinkedIn is a no-brainer, let me share with you three powerful examples of just how useful LinkedIn can be for you (and we haven't even discussed yet the goodies you get with Facebook and Twitter!).

These three examples assume you've been actively using LinkedIn for four to six months and have fifty to one hundred first-level connections. Remember, everyone on LI started out with no connections. You'd be surprised how many people you know, and how delighted they will be to hear from you and connect with you on LI.

In Chapter 8 I'll share with you a memory jogger to help you recall people's names so you can invite them to connect with you.

LinkedIn Situation 1:

Problem: You have been unemployed for three months and are scraping the bottom of the barrel for job leads. You have been faithfully network-ing, but to no avail.

Solution: On your LI homepage there is a text box where you can type and send a short message (140 characters limit) to all of your connections at once. Let's say you have seventy-five connections. In less than five minutes you can contact all seventy-five of your connections with the following message:

"My job search is bucking some serious headwinds. Could sure use your help with a few job leads, ideas, or referrals. Thanks for your help."

This message effectively communicates to your private network your situation in a quick-read fashion without annoying anyone. Even if you recently contacted many of these people, it keeps your name in front of them.

Upon receipt of your message, expect about 10 percent of your connections to respond as follows:

- Forward your LI profile to a trusted friend or associate endorsing you
- Email you back with a job lead, suggestion, or other useful information
- Call you to chat

Comments: It's perfectly OK to call those who didn't respond to your message. Don't make the mistake of trying to figure out why someone didn't respond to you. You're not a mind reader and you never know what is going on in somebody's life. Maybe they get 50-100 emails a day and simply can't get through them all. Maybe they're traveling and are behind on following up.

Maybe their dog died.

The important thing to remember is most people want to help others, especially friends and former associates. If your email was read, you will be on their mind when you call. Sometimes it will take two or three follow up calls, spaced over a couple of months, before some folks will oblige you.

Pearl of Wisdom: Lack of follow up can be costly. Heed this wise old saying: *Much is lost for the want of asking.* Don't let your fear prevent you from having a conversation with someone.

LinkedIn Situation 2:

Problem: An outstanding company in your industry has a job posting on their website with your name written all over it. How do you get your resume in front of the hiring authority versus emailing it into the Human Resources' black hole?

Solution: On your LI homepage, go to the search box in the top right-hand corner. Click the down arrow to reveal, "Companies". Enter the name of the company. Most mid-to-large size companies have a profile page on LI with a concise company overview. Here is the best part. It not only shows you the names of your first level connections who currently work there, but it also reveals the names of anyone who is connected to your first level contacts.

Wow!

In other words, your first level connection Wendy doesn't work there, but she just happens to be connected to Suzie Q, the engineering director.

You now have a golden opportunity to do one of the following:

- Email or call Wendy and ask her if she would introduce you to Suzie.
- Write an email to Suzie, but forward it first to Wendy asking her to pass it along to Suzie with her endorsement of you. LI has a nifty template to do this with a hyperlink back to your professional profile page so Wendy and Suzie can pop up your resume/profile on their screen with a simple mouse click. Very, *very* cool.

Imagine getting a personal email or phone call from Suzie Q requesting your resume. When she receives it, she promptly picks up the phone and instructs the HR manager to set up an interview. The poor guy who applied on line is still waiting for any kind of acknowledgment that his resume was received, let alone an invitation to interview.

Do you see the power of leap-frogging over Human Resources and going straight to the decision maker? Expect to be treated as "a candidate on the short list" by everyone involved in your interview because *the boss* received your resume through a referral from one of her friends—*very* powerful stuff.

This strategy even works if you know a lower level staff person at this company. If a respected staff person refers you to the hiring manager, you're ten times more likely to be interviewed, or at least have your resume read by the ultimate decision maker. Many companies today even pay their employees a small bonus ($500-1,000) for referrals they hire. That's a pretty good incentive for someone to put in a good word for you and pass along your resume.

A recent survey of corporations revealed that 27 percent of their hiring comes thru referrals, or one in four. This is huge and can't be ignored. LI connects you with tons of influential people who can be your advocate instead of relying on a wing and prayer.

LinkedIn Situation 3:

Problem: You are currently employed, but rumors abound that your company is losing a major account and layoffs are possible. You can't afford to be laid off, but your work schedule limits your job search activities.

Solution: Since you've been consistently inviting people to connect with you on LI over the past six to twelve months, you now have two hundred first level connections. Each of them is connected to approximately one hundred people, expanding your second level connections to two thousand people. Each of them is connected to one hundred people, expanding your third level connections to twenty thousand people.

Since you now know that 70 percent of all successful job searches come through referrals, you don't waste your time on the major job boards, but instead, quietly go about your job search by simply networking with your connections.

Hey you really do have connections!

For less than an hour a day, you can network with trusted friends and associates and their trusted contacts to open a door for you, refer you to someone, or email you with any job leads that come along.

Studies have consistently shown that referrals as deep as three levels are almost as potent as first level referrals. In other words, you call your first level connection Jeff for help finding a job. Jeff can't directly help you, but he refers you to his friend Rob and tells him you're one of the good guys.

When you talk to Rob, the conversation is much more relaxed and friendly since you both are friends with Jeff.

Unfortunately, Rob isn't able to help, but he refers you to his good friend, Sarah, and tells her you must be good if Jeff said so. When Sarah picks up the phone, you are received warmly. Just so happens that Sarah's company is looking for someone just like you. She gladly goes up the mountain with your resume to the right people.

Isn't it amazing that Sarah doesn't know you from the man-in-the-moon and she's treating you like royalty? That's the power of networking.

But most people are slow to change and won't take time every day—or at least a couple of times a week—to grow and nurture their network. Don't make this mistake. It's important that you manage your career in good and bad times. LinkedIn not only makes it easier to find people, it allows you to stay connected forever because it's in everyone's best interest to keep their profile current.

One last thing about LI before we move on:

Networking is a two-way street. You must provide value to others if you expect help in return. The best way to do this is after your learning curve and initial push to get connected to as many people as possible, devote thirty minutes a day to browsing your network.

Get involved in groups and provide comments and advice in your area of expertise. This keeps you visible and credible to your connections. Always help your connections with a referral or lead if they reach out to you. Return emails and voice mails promptly.

We live in an incredible day and age where nothing stays the same. Change is inevitable. Simply put, we all need each other to be successful and secure. Social networking tools like LinkedIn provide us with a powerful way to do this.

The best LinkedIn training for job seekers is provided by Jason Alba. You can read about him and his services at: http://www.linkedin.com/in/jasonalba.

In October 2010, I attended intermediate and advanced LinkedIn training from Jason and was *very* impressed. Jason is not only an expert on LI, but an excellent teacher and speaker.

Note: LinkedIn is a business. From time to time they change their policies and practices. The features I described to you are free; however, this may not always be the case. If some of their free features are switched to premium features, it might be worth it to upgrade. Reputable sites like LinkedIn usually charge a reasonable monthly fee for their premium features.

Facebook: The best place to make friends with your business connections

In February 2004, Facebook launched from the Harvard dorm room of co-founders Mark Zuckerberg, Dustin Moskovitz, Chris Hughes and Eduardo Saverin. Facebook was created as a way for Harvard students to stay in touch, but shortly after it launched they expanded their network to included Stanford, Columbia and Yale. By year's end, they had one million subscribers, and Facebook went viral.

Today (2011), Facebook has over 600 million subscribers and is the number two ranked website in the world. Google is ranked number one.

You might be asking yourself the following questions:

1. I already have a FB account and really like it. Isn't FB for friends and family, and LinkedIn for business?
2. With all the great features of LinkedIn, do I really need FB to help me with my job search? What's the difference?
3. Is spending time on FB really a good use of my time when I desperately need a job?
4. A few family members and friends post silly comments and pictures on my FB. Won't this hurt my job prospects if hiring managers see them?

All of these questions and concerns are valid and I'll discuss them in a minute. But here is the main reason why you can't ignore FB as part of your job search strategy.

Do I need to say it again?

Seventy percent of the most effective job search methods are networking oriented. The best way to find current and past co-workers, bosses, leaders, suppliers, customers, friends, and other business partners—who you value and trust—is through LinkedIn and Facebook. Most of these contacts are going to have a presence on one, or both, of these websites. Simply put, it's the fastest and most efficient way to get in touch, and stay in touch with people.

Facebook is a networking tool, and with 600 million users, it won't be long before the entire planet is on Facebook.

So, let's get back to your questions:

1. I already have a FB account and really like it. Isn't FB for friends and family, and LinkedIn for business?

Answer: Yes and no. You can use FB for both and limit what visitors see about you. You can create an attractive public profile, so when prospective employers look for you on FB, they are greeted with a professional image and a positive impression of you. And believe me, HR and hiring managers will look you up. If you're not on LinkedIn or Facebook, or if you have a half-baked profile, employers will conclude you're not in step with the times.

2. With all the great features of LinkedIn, do I really need Facebook to help me with my job search? What's the difference?

Answer: Facebook is more interactive and conversational than LinkedIn. It is also warmer, friendlier, and more casual in nature. FB has 6 times the number of users as LI. Recent studies reveal that people spend a significant amount of time on FB. Fifty percent of their users log on daily. Facebook is the best place to meet and make friends with your business connections.

Also, friends and other important people in your life can more easily find you if you're out there.

You want to be found.

Facebook allows you to segregate your friends (connections) into several groups (lists). This allows you to control who can post comments in your space or who can see your comments.

Example of lists: Family, College Buddies, Business Associates, College Alumni, Church Friends, Hockey Team.

3. Is spending time on FB really a good use of my time when I desperately need a job?

Answer: Absolutely! Once you get beyond the learning curve of FB, you should be able to spend less than an hour a day networking on it. The most time consuming part is creating a good profile, and finding people to connect with. You can also join interactive groups, including good job networking groups. Check out the hundreds of applications available to you on FB that will simplify how you source information and stay up to date.

4. A few family members and friends post silly comments and pictures on my FB. Won't this hurt my job prospects if hiring managers see them?

Answer: Yes…if you give the public open access to your information—which I can't imagine any sane person doing. Fortunately, FB allows you to customize your privacy settings to control how much of your personal information is accessible to outsiders and even friends who are already connected with you on FB. You can also block knuckleheaded family members and kids from bombarding you with non-stop nonsense…*without* them knowing it.

Twitter: *Your very own radio station on the Internet*

I have to admit, when I first landed on Twitter's home page, I couldn't figure out for the life of me what all the fuss was about it.

Who hasn't heard of Twitter? But what is it?

You can only type a message with a maximum of 140 characters which counts spaces, symbols, and letters as one character. How can anyone benefit from such a short message?

Well, I'm here to tell you, you can. I am now a die-hard Twitter fan! After several days of fumbling through it, I get it. The light bulb finally came on.

Picture in your mind a gymnasium. As you walk in the door and scan the gym, you notice in each corner of the room a gathering of friendly people. Each group seems to be having a good time. People are talking, sharing information, and occasionally laughing.

Each group appears warm and inviting.

There is a banner over each group in the room. One banner reads: **Career Advice**. Another banner reads: **Resumes 101**. Still another banner reads: **Job Seekers**.

Since you're troubled about the quality of your resume, you decide to join the Resumes 101 group. You are greeted warmly and meet a couple of people who are professional resume writers. They give you some great ideas. You also talk with one or two HR managers who tell you what their pet peeves are about resumes.

As luck would have it, one of those mistakes is on your current resume!

After awhile, you decide to wander over to the Job Seekers group. Although this is a friendly bunch, one of the job seekers is discouraged about their job search. You share with them a website full of ideas to rekindle their enthusiasm. You also know of a company in their field that recently announced they will be doing a lot of hiring in the coming months.

Welcome to the virtual world of Twitter.

The benefit of Twitter is the ability to connect with people from all over the world on a daily basis, who just might have special knowledge to help you solve your problems…including lack of gainful employment.

It's networking with a heart.

Everyone has a gift to give you, and Twitter is a fantastic way for people to present their gifts to one another. It is a true testimony to the wise old saying, *"The more you give, the more you get."*

Here is a micro-lesson on Twitter to enlighten you further:

- Twitter is like being on a CB radio, text conversations with real people in real time.
- You can join in these conversations to share ideas, web links, humor, and inspiration.
- If you can text on your cell phone, you can effectively use Twitter.
- Twitter is like having your very own radio station with fans who *want* to follow you.
- You can follow other people's "stations" to learn about their ideas, inspiration, and links to fresh cutting-edge information.
- Lots of employers, recruiters, and other influential people hang out on Twitter…sort of like gathering around the water cooler at the office. It's the "in thing" to do.
- If you have a presence on Twitter, your attractiveness to hiring authorities will increase, as you are seen as someone who is up to snuff and in step with the times.
- You never know whom you might bump into out there in the virtual world. All kinds of people are watching…including employers and other powerful people. The more you interact and connect with people, the faster you will find a job.

Here is the fastest way to start using Twitter for your job search:

- Go to: http://www.twitter.com, and sign up for a free account.
- Make sure you use your real name for your User Name or a variation. Example: MikePetras or MPetras.

- Post a professional looking photo of yourself, not an avatar, logo, or symbol.
- Once on Twitter, read the Help section to learn their unique language and other useful tips. It takes a little time to get it, but you'll catch on fast.
- To get followers, simply start following other people.
- If you follow me, I'll follow you back. My Username is @MikePetras. However, if you share inappropriate topics or don't post your photo, I probably won't follow you.
- After you follow me, go to my followers and follow eight or nine of them. Most of them will follow you back.
- Don't go overboard with following others just to get followers. You want people to follow you naturally as much as possible.
- Be real. People want to connect with real people who add value to the Twitter community.
- The best way to grasp the Twitter culture is to simply read the Tweets (messages) of those you're following.
- Download TweetDeck (www.TweetDeck.com) to help you better follow and navigate.
- Once you are set up on TweetDeck, click on the + sign at the top of the page and add the following columns to connect you with professional career advisors, fellow job seekers, executive recruiters, HR managers, and other influential people. Don't forget to use the hash sign (#)...which is part of the Twitter language:
  - #hirefriday
  - #HFChat
  - #career
  - #careeradvice
  - #jobhunt
  - #jobhuntchat
  - #jobsearch
  - #jobseeker
  - #jobs
  - #interview
  - #workwednesday

- As of this writing (March 2011), the above eleven Twitter locations are the best places for job seekers to tweet (text/instant message) and discover people who have the power to help you by either providing advice, hope, inspiration, encouragement, or cutting edge employment trends. You will also help others which is empowering and gratifying.

- Here is another very cool Twitter activity. Several groups will meet at designated times during the week to chat live. For example, #HFChat (Hire Friday Chat) meets online every Friday from 12:00 to 1:00 PM ET. Two or three employment problems are presented to the group to solve. Sometimes over one hundred people participate in these live events. Usually these discussions are published in an on-line newsletter to refer to later. Here is a link showing the schedules of several Twitter group by topic: https://spreadsheets.google.com/ccc?key=ruaz3GZveOsoXUO Ot86B3AQ#gid=0

Words to the wise about using Twitter:

- Don't be negative, lewd, rude, or crude. All your tweets are public and search-able.
- Try to connect with people off line via telephone or email.
- Don't be a whiner or complainer. People come to Twitter seeking hope and solutions.
- Point people to useful links, books, and gurus; they will reciprocate.
- Twitter has its fair share of knuckleheads, spammers, and self-promoters. Just ignore them. You'll still find nuggets of gold. Rise above the noise by being professional.

True story: I bumped into a CEO on Twitter and received a surprise call

I was using TweetDeck to participate in a #HFChat discussion (Hire Friday Chat) with at least one hundred people about best job search practices. It was a great discussion in real time. TweetDeck gives you the ability to communicate with many people in a discussion group, but also provides you with the flexibility to monitor three or four other groups at the same time.

Simply by chance, I glanced over at one of the other groups and read the following tweet: *"I'll hit the brakes and they'll fly right by us."* Does that line from a famous movie ring a bell for you movie buffs?

It's from the movie *Top Gun*, and it was uttered by Tom Cruise (call sign *Maverick*) during a dog fight scene. I had no idea who sent that tweet or why, but just for the heck of it, I hit my reply button and said: *"And I got your wing, Maverick!"*

Next thing you know, I get a tweet from this person who asks for my opinion about a job related article on TalentZoo.com (popular online niche job board). I quickly linked over to the article and read it. It was an excellent article about questions job seekers should ask in their interviews.

I replied back to this person that I was very impressed with the article and thanked him for sharing it with me. A few minutes later I thought to myself, who was that guy? So, I clicked on his profile and discovered it was Rick Myers, Founder and CEO of TalentZoo.

Fast forward two weeks.

I received an email from Rick Myers' content editor inviting me to write an article for TalentZoo about midlife careers to be prominently featured on their website. I was flattered by their invitation and immediately accepted. This opportunity provided me with great exposure as an author, professional career advisor, and executive recruiter. It also drove traffic to my website, job-interview-wisdom.com.

Twitter can put you at the right place, at the right time, and expose you to people you would never associate with otherwise. You never know who might by impressed by one of your tweets and decide to check you out or refer you to one of their powerful friends.

In summary: Social networking is one of the best ways to stay connected with trusted friends and associates. It is also a great way to meet influential people. Although it is an exciting new way to network, *do not stop* job hunting for the next three to six weeks while you learn each SN site and tweak them to perfection.

Gradually phase in these SN tools and slowly make them part of your daily routine. Social networking is only a tool. It is not the silver bullet to end all of your job search hassles.

Too many job seekers hide behind email, Facebook, LinkedIn, Twitter, or other passive ways to nurture their relationships. Some job seekers even expect people to be mind readers and are frustrated when few, if any, of their friends reach out to them during their unemployment trial.

These tools will never replace the personal touch. The best way to connect with people is still in person, or over the phone. Actually *talking* with people is the best networking strategy...which brings us to the next chapter along our job search journey.

Chapter 8:
The Art of Networking by Making Warm Calls

We should be taught not to wait for inspiration to start a thing.
Action always generates inspiration.
Inspiration seldom generates action.
~Frank Tibolt

You've arrived at a significant turning point in your job search. You've made it through job search boot camp, and are better prepared to step onto the battlefield.

In the remaining chapters, I want to share with you the best ways to go about executing your job search strategy. We're going to build your contact list and learn how to approach people for support without annoying them or sounding like a job beggar.

Networking is by far the best way to find a job, but most people resist doing it because they fear people will be put off by their call. Also, it's a humbling experience to ask people for help.

Whatever your fear and hesitation, these next action steps literally hold the power to turn your situation around.

In the US Navy, you have to know how to swim to graduate from boot camp. For those who don't know how to swim, it's a terrifying experience to jump into deep water off the deck of a ship. Poor swimmers literally have to be dragged into the water at first.

There is a saying in the Navy to conjure up courage in the face of fear: ***"Action cures fear."***

Remember those words the first time you pick up the phone to call one of your contacts. The first two or three calls will be awkward. The phone will feel like it weighs one hundred pounds. But each call thereafter will get easier and easier.

After you've made twenty to twenty-five calls, you'll not only feel an immense sense of accomplishment, but you'll wonder what all the fuss was about.

How to build a huge network of contacts

1. Here is the best way to jog your memory for the names of all your past friends and associates who already know, respect, and trust you. Block out sixty to ninety minutes of uninterrupted time. Sit down in a quiet place and write down the following categories which define your past relationships with people:
    a. Friends (including childhood, Boy Scouts, high school, college, athletics, clubs, fraternities, military)
    b. Neighbors (past and present)
    c. Fellow church members (even if you don't attend regularly)
    d. Family (cousins, aunts, uncles, brothers, sisters, children, parents)
    e. Parents of your kid's soccer team, choir group, or other activities
    f. Past work associates at all levels (secretaries, administrators, managers, executives)
    g. Former customers, suppliers, retailers, distributors, sales people
    h. Former bosses
    i. Bankers, accountants, lawyers (these people are *always* well connected to numerous business owners and executives)
    j. Business advisors (insurance professionals, realtors, consultants, trainers, teachers, executive recruiters)
    k. Groups: golf, hobby, Masons, community service, hunting, fishing, sports
    l. Can you think of any other categories?

2. Now write down the names of everyone you know under the above categories. It doesn't matter if you don't know where they live or how to contact them. **Important:** Don't prejudge your past connections. Just start writing down names as soon as they pop into your mind. We're simply brainstorming right now. It might

help to refer to your HS yearbook, an old company directory, or a photo album. If you can't think of someone's name just write down anything that will help you recall their name later. Afterwards, you might want to call an old friend to help you fill in the blanks or help you recollect someone.

Pearl of Wisdom: You never know who someone might know. Your best friend in the Camp Fire Girls—who you haven't spoken to in twenty years—might be a leader with a growing enterprise. She will probably be overjoyed to hear from you, and could refer you to her powerful friends or even get you a job where she works. The humblest person you know may be connected to someone who can open *big* doors for you.

---

3. Set up a free membership on LinkedIn and Facebook. This is the fastest and easiest way to find the majority of your past associates and friends. It's also an excellent way to nurture these relationships on a professional basis from now on. See the last chapter on social networking for benefits of LinkedIn, Facebook, and Twitter, including links to "how to" sites to learn each application as painlessly as possible.

Call everyone on your network list (see sample script below). Be warm and personable, but get right to the point. Tell them you are out of work and need their help. See if they will share with you the names of two or three people who may be in a position to either hire you or provide you with referrals to network with.

If your list of first level connections is thirty people, and everyone on your list gives you two names, you now have a list of ninety people. When you contact these second level referrals, the snowball grows. It's only a matter of time before you literally stumble upon an opportunity.

Your initial approach to someone should be on the phone. If you don't know someone's phone number, go the extra mile to try to find it. If after a reasonable effort you can't get a phone number, go ahead and email them or send them a type written letter.

Special Tip: If you can't find someone on one of the SN sites, look them up on 411.com. Sometimes 411.co will only show an address, but no phone number. This is probably because your contact doesn't have a land line. They just use their cell phone. In this case, mail them a letter. Keep your letter short, but personal. It's not a good idea to enclose your resume. Make a connection first. At this early stage of your networking, you're looking to reconnect and get information. Not only that, it's not a good idea to have your resume floating around all over the place. Only share it with people who ask you for it or who are in a position to hire you.

When you call someone for help and they don't respond warmly, don't over analyze it. You never know what burdens people are caring around. Maybe they're just having a bad day.

True story: It's easy to misjudge others

Linda was friends with Martha, a co-worker who didn't have a very good marriage. Linda invited Martha to attend church with her. Martha accepted, but asked Linda if she would mind picking up her and her two young children because they only had one car. Martha also said she probably wouldn't' be able to attend church every Sunday.

Linda agreed to do this even though Martha lived a considerable distance out of the way.

Over the next six months, Martha would call Linda once or twice a month and ask her for a ride to church. Linda always agreed, but gradually became annoyed that Martha always seemed to call at the last minute. Every time she picked up Martha, they were at least ten minutes late to church.

Linda was always punctual and hated to be late.

Linda complained to her husband about it. *"Why can't Martha be more considerate of my time? I go out of my way to pick her up and she doesn't have the courtesy to simply be on time. And why does she always call me at the last minute?"*

"I've just about had it," Linda quipped.

A couple of weeks later, as Linda was driving Martha and her kids home from church, Martha said, *"You know Linda, I can't tell you how much I appreciate you driving us to church. It really helps me get through the week. I'm really sorry I call you at the last minute. But my husband is very temperamental and volatile. The littlest things can set him off. I'm frightened of him and don't know quite what to do about it.*

So, I make sure on Sunday mornings he has his coffee, paper, and breakfast... and then when he seems to be in a pretty good mood, I ask him if it would be alright if I took the kids to church. Most of the time he says no, but once or twice a month he lets us go. I call you right away, hoping you haven't already left for church. You're such a good friend, Linda."

Pearl of Wisdom: Whenever we are stressed or frustrated, we tend to misjudge other's intentions. We take things too personally. We overreact to little things like not getting a return phone call, or lack of help from someone we admire. Truth is...life sometimes gets in the way for all of us—including friends and hiring authorities. Resist prejudging people's intentions. This knowledge is liberating and helps you move forward despite someone's poor attitude.

How to approach people without annoying them to get what you need

Just read this script for now. We'll go over why it works in a few minutes. Pay particular attention to the questions in **bold italics**.

You: Hi John, this is Mike Petras calling—a voice from the past, I'm sure.

John: Mike! How the heck are you?! Man, it's been awhile. How are Beth and the kids?

You: Good. Everyone is doing well. We're living in South Bend now, but still have pleasant memories of our time together at XYZ Corp.

John: We didn't know how good we had it back then. Times have sure changed—that's for sure! So, to what do I owe the honor of your call?

You: Well...I'm hoping you can help me with my job search and give me some good advice. (**Comment:** Get right to the point. Ask for help. Most people want to help others. People like having their ego stroked by someone asking them for their advice.)
I was downsized from ABC Corp as their Sales Manager a few months ago, and I've been actively looking for a similar position. But it's been tough sledding. *Is there any hiring going on in your company for someone with my background?*

John: Gosh, Mike, I sure wish I could help you out, but we've been on a hiring freeze for the past year due to this stubborn economy. You're welcome to email to me your resume and I'll pass it along to our HR folks. (**Comment:** Always agree, but don't get your hopes up. John is just being nice and trying to help. HR already has piles of resumes and yours will get thrown on the pile and not even read since they have no urgency to hire right now. Sometimes your resume won't even get out of John's email inbox. Even so, keep playing the game. Thank him, agree to it, but continue to probe John with the questions below. Your goal is to try to get something from every call...information, referrals, job leads. Remember this slogan: *everyone has a gift to give you.* If you ask the right way, you're more likely to get some useful information that you can act upon today. Keep reading.)

You: OK...sure, thanks. What's your email address? [pause] *John...are you aware of any hiring going on at one of your competitors, or any other good companies in your area?*

John: Umm...not that I can think of...ah...no, not really.

You: *Have you been contacted by any recruiters recently about job opportunities?* (**Comments:** If so, get the name and number of this recruiter. Call them up and tell them John referred you to them. This is a win-win-win situation. Recruiters like it when someone they recently contacted refers someone to them. Networking is the way most good recruiters work. So, right off the bat John is viewed favorably by the recruiter. Also, you might be able to give this recruiter some referrals of people you know to help with their search for candidates. The recruiter may not be able to help you personally, but might refer you to one of his associates or contacts. Most recruiters are well connected and if you try and help them, they'll return the favor.)

John: No, John. I haven't been approached by an executive recruiter for quite awhile.

You: ***Do you know of anyone else I can network with who may be able to give me a lead or a referral—a supplier, customer—or even one of our former co-workers?***

John: Yeah...give my friend, Rocky Balboa, a call. He is the sales VP with Free Fall Elevators in Duluth, Minnesota. Good guy...great leader. I don't know if they're hiring or not, but I hear Duluth has great ice fishing through June. HaHaHaHa! (**Comments:** Thankfully accept John's referral. And yes, call Rocky Balboa even if Duluth is the last place on earth you'd move to. You never know who Rocky may know or what life-changing information he could share with you. And another thing, if there is a job in Duluth for you, what do you have to lose by checking it out? You can always turn down a job offer. If you're unemployed, never prejudge anything. It never hurts to talk and check it out. Maybe the divine hand of providence is calling you to Duluth for a very special reason.)

You: Thanks a lot, John! I'll give Rocky a call. One last thing before we say good bye...***do you have any advice for me about my job search?***

John: Hang in there Mike, and blah, blah, blah...

Pearl of Wisdom: The reason you ask people specific questions is because it helps jog their memory. Most people want to help, but may not be able to think of a referral off the cuff, especially if their mind is on their work when you called them. Always try to get at least one referral of someone who may be able to help you, even if it's only to network with them. This way you will double or triple your list of contacts. Studies have shown conclusively that these second and third tier referrals are just as willing to help you as one of your friends, former co-workers, or acquaintances. The reason for this is because when you use someone's name, it immediately builds trust and people drop their defenses. This is powerful. Put this to work for you on a daily basis.

True story: Good networking technique disarms age discrimination

Mel, a fifty-nine year old engineering manager, struggled for months to find a job with no results. He had a stellar background, wonderful personality, and ethics beyond reproach. The real reason he was only getting a handful of interviews was because most companies wanted to hire a younger person.

Yep...flat out age discrimination.

Even so, Mel methodically networked each day using the warm calling script outlined above. One day, one of his contacts referred him to an executive recruiter. Mel called this recruiter and it turned out that Mel was a good candidate for a job search the recruiter was conducting.

The recruiter submitted his resume to his client company, but it was rejected for flimsy reasons.

Hmm...too old?

The recruiter pressed the company to interview Mel because he lived local—and more importantly—met or exceeded all of their hiring requirements. The recruiter also took the liberty to call one of Mel's references who provided a glowing report even his mom would have been proud of. He submitted this reference in writing to his client company and flat out asked them why Mel wasn't worthy of an interview.

After fumbling around and failing to come up with a good reason, the company relented and agreed to interview Mel. Despite fierce competition from younger candidates, Mel interviewed very well and was offered the job.

Moral of the story: You are much more likely to win job interviews and receive job offers if you have an advocate on the inside to remove roadblocks for you. Your advocate may just come through a friend of a friend. So, make those calls and continue to expand your network.

You can never have too many friends.

True story: Lousy location leads to early promotion and job security

In a prior life I applied for a job in Carbondale, Pennsylvania.

Ever been to Carbondale? Well, let me put it to you this way: it's not exactly Shangri-La.

Carbondale is a decaying coal town of nine thousand people just north of Scranton. My drive to the interview took me by abandon strip mines with rusty mining machinery perched on a ravaged landscape. Most of the houses and buildings were built in the 1930's and hadn't been updated since.

I almost did a U-turn in the middle of the road and laid down rubber for home.

But I proceeded with my interview and was delighted to find out that twenty minutes from the office was a quaint ski village called The Village of Four Seasons. There were several chalets for rent and the community was designed after a small village in Switzerland. I couldn't believe my eyes when I checked out the place. It was a far cry from the war torn ambiance of Carbondale.

I also discovered the upscale communities of Clarks Summit and Waverly, both about a thirty minute commute. When I factored in our proximity to the Pocono Mountains and only a two hour car ride to New York City, things starting looking better.

You see, what attracted me to Carbondale was the job. It was a great job with excellent career potential. The location is what scared me. But rather than just turn my nose up at a great opportunity because of the location, I decided to check it out for myself. I'm glad I did.

I ended up taking the job. We moved to The Village of Four Seasons. To this day we have pleasant memories of our sojourn there. My children were young at the time and we spent a lot of time together fishing, hiking, sledding, and enjoying nature. We still talk about it.

This move literally catapulted my career. Prior to taking this position, the company could not retain sales managers because of the location and the company's track record of poor quality products. Like clockwork the sales manager position turned over every year. Since I had already solved the location crisis by living up at The Village, all I had to do now was perform well.

I reasoned that this company had nowhere to go but up since I couldn't screw it up any worse. Their parent company was strong financially and committed to turning it around. Frankly, I was excited about the challenge and confident I could make a difference.

Fast forward two years.

This operation was forced to close due to an unforeseen economic recession, along with ten other operations in North America. Since I was a short-timer with this company, I expected to be laid off. To my surprise, I was laterally moved to another location. When the recession ended two years later, I was promoted to regional sales director. At the time I was one of the youngest regional directors in the company ($800 million in sales).

If I hadn't taken the Carbondale job, I never would have received this promotion. The company didn't forget my positive efforts to turn around their struggling Carbondale operation. I enjoyed a rewarding career and thank my lucky stars I didn't do a U-turn on my initial visit to lovely Carbondale.

When you are unemployed, explore *every* opportunity. Keep an open mind and get all the facts before making a decision. You might just hit the lottery.

Good follow- up habits often lead to bonus referrals and new information

After you talk to someone's referrals and follow up on their leads, shoot them a quick email update. Make it warm and personal:

"Hi David, I spoke with June Cleaver yesterday. She didn't know of any job openings in my field, but gave me two referrals with solid potential. Appreciate your help. Hope the rest of your week goes well."

This keeps your name in front of your contact and makes it easy for them to contact you if they come up with another lead or referral. Make sure all your contact information—especially your cell phone number—is in the email. Make it as easy as possible for them to get a hold of you.

Call everyone in your network every three to four weeks, *even* if they gave you two or three names the last time you called. It's always best to call them rather than email them. Let them know you are still on the job market and ask them if they have any new leads or information for you. Most people want to help, but everyone has a lot on their plate these days.

Don't assume people will remember you are looking for a job after you called them once. After you've contacted them two or three times, they will be more likely to remember that you are earnestly looking for a job. This is just one of the ugly truths about human nature. We simply need to be reminded a lot. My wife will verify this.

Chapter 9:
The Art of Networking by Making Cold Calls

I am looking for a lot of men who have an infinite capacity to not know what can't be done.
~Henry Ford

Networking through friends and past associates is affectionately referred to as "warm calling." That's what we just talked about in the last chapter. It sure beats the heck out of cold calling.

As everyone knows, cold calling is simply calling someone you don't know, out of the blue, and asking them for something like information, leads, referrals, and so on. Most people—even seasoned sales people—hate doing it.

Believe it or not…it works.

And, it would be in your best interest to give it try, or learn how to do it more effectively if you've tried it in the past with little success. Now, before you skip over this chapter while muttering to yourself, *"I'm not doing this"*, first find out why it works, and what you can do to actually warm it up a bit.

What have you got to lose?

You've tried the job boards, shot gunning out your resume by the truck loads, and other conventional search methods to no avail. So, you're reading this book to learn new ways of doing things because, well, you want your life back and you're sick and tired of being unemployed, in a job you hate, or stuck in a career going nowhere.

Cold calling will be uncomfortable at first, but once you know how best to go about it, you'll be amazed at how friendly and pleasant total strangers respond to you.

6 benefits of cold calling and why it's worth doing

1. Empowers you to leapfrog over *"the system"*
2. Invigorates your current job search when nothing else seems to be working
3. Gives you fresh courage and tears down the walls of fear and procrastination
4. Provides an effective way for you to approach companies you would love to work for *regardless* of whether or not they have a job opening
5. Proactive job search approach vs. reactive approach
6. The success rate of cold calling is much higher than answering ads, mailing resumes, and other passive job methods

True story: Unconventional job search approach wins job offer

Steve was a quality manager for a small privately owned manufacturer. The owner, Karl, had known Steve for years, and recruited him to his company with the promise of Steve taking over as general manager so Karl could semi-retire and finally enjoy the fruits of his labor.

After five years it became apparent that Karl couldn't let go of the reins of his company.

Despite this disappointment, Steve liked his job and enjoyed his relationship with the owner. So, he hung in there figuring when the time was right everything would work out.

One day, Karl walked into Steve's office, quietly closed the door, and calmly told Steve he was letting him go.

Steve's jaw hit the floor.

He felt betrayed since he had been so trusting of Karl and loyal to him over the years.

Karl's comments that Steve's dismissal was for financial reasons—not his performance—did little to calm Steve's nerves as he pondered how he was going to take care of his wife and four children. To make matters worse, Karl did *not* offer Steve *any* kind of severance pay.

Steve looked for a job by visiting all of the over-hyped job boards like Monster, CareerBuilder, Hot Jobs, and a few others.

Nothing.

After weeks of looking for a job this way, getting nowhere fast, and having no income stream, Steve started getting desperate. So, he called his good friend, Matt, a small business owner with lots of connections in the community.

Steve shared with Matt how he was thrown under the bus by his past employer, and asked Matt if he knew of any companies out there that might be hiring.

Matt paused to think, but told him nothing really came to mind. But here is how the rest of the conversation went:

Matt: Have you tried calling Rinky Dink Manufacturing? They seem to always be hiring.

Steve: Where are they located?

Matt: About thirty minutes from here over in Hicksville. Why don't you just drive over there in the morning and find out if they're hiring?

Steve: Are you kidding me, man? Just drive over there, walk in the lobby, and ask for a quality manager job?

Matt: Yeah. Why not?

Steve: That's going to go over like a screen door in a submarine, Matt. All I'm going to do is annoy them and then they'll probably just send me out to their website to apply online.

Matt: How do you know? What have you got to lose? Just do it, Steve. You think too much.

Steve: Nothin', I guess. I'm so desperate I'll try just about anything once, but this sounds like a big drill. Whatever...

Fast forward two weeks. Telephone rings over at Matt's house. Let's listen in:

Matt: Hello

Steve: Are you a psychic, Matt?

Matt: Hey, Steve, what's up? What did you say?

Steve: I said are you psychic?

Matt: What are you talking about?

Steve: Guess where I am now working?

Matt: I don't know. Where?

Steve: Rinky Dink Mfg as their new quality manager!

Matt: Seriously?!

Steve: Would I lie?

Matt: Tell me about it.

Steve: Well, remember a couple of weeks ago when you told me to just pop in at Rinky Dink Mfg to see if they were hiring?

Matt: Yeah.

Steve: Even though I thought it was a waste of time, I did it. When I walked in the door I told the receptionist that I was a quality manager looking for a job and I'd like to speak with their general manager. The receptionist then asked me if I was here for my interview. I told her I didn't have an appointment. She then informed me they had a quality manager opening and were actively interviewing for the position. She told me to hold on while she called the general manager. In a few minutes he came out and greeted me in the lobby. He invited me back to his office. He went over my resume and actually did a short job interview with me. I was shocked. He then invited me back for a second interview with him and several other managers. To make a long story short, I was offered the job the next week and eagerly accepted. Thank you, Matt. You're a genius!

Matt: Thanks, Steve, but, quite frankly, I had no clue Rinky Dink was hiring.

Note: This really is a true story. I didn't just make this up (except the name Rinky Dink Mfg).

Pearl of Wisdom: Everyone has a gift to give you. It may be one tiny piece of information that leads you to someone who knows about a job opening. Often times opportunities are laid right at our feet, but our flawed understanding of *how things should be done* prevent us from taking action. Don't make that mistake. Getting a job offer is nothing more than putting yourself in the right place at the right time with your best game face on. This involves connecting with as many people as possible on a regular basis. The more you reach out to people, the greater your odds of landing a job. The more you isolate yourself and hide behind the Internet or other passive ways to find a job, the harder it will be to find something.

Why strangers won't give you a hard time when you call them

As an executive recruiter I make a ton of cold calls. I'm always trying to gain new client companies and connect with excellent job seekers. I've been in the trenches a long time.

One thing has always amazed me.

After fifteen years of cold calling, I can count on one hand the number of times someone hung up on me or said something rude to me. That's pretty amazing when you consider I am interrupting people in the middle of their work day to sell them on my recruiting services. When someone does hang up on me, or says something stupid—which is extremely rare—I actually laugh about it…and then, just make my next call.

You see, I've learned over the years that most people are good, honest, hard-working folks who are just like you and me. These days a lot of folks either have been on the receiving end of misfortune or know someone who has. Most people not only want to help others, they are happy to do it.

The secret to getting help from people is all in your approach to them. So, I'm going to walk you through my cold calling script and explain to you along the way the psychology going on. Please feel free to copy and use it.

Why building a call list gives you courage, confidence, and momentum

The hardest part of cold calling is figuring out whom to call. The fastest way to do this is by accessing an online directory of companies called ReferenceUSA (more on how to gain free access to this great resource in a minute). Before we go there, it's important you understand why building your call list will give you the courage and confidence you need to actually make those tough calls.

When you put together a call list of twenty to twenty-five companies you set yourself up to make one call right after another in rapid succession. This consistent action creates momentum, like a big tail wind pushing you forward.

Momentum is a powerful force of nature that defies explanation. All of us have experienced it at least once in our lives. When the force of momentum is with you, everything just seems to click. Some call it being in the groove. You know exactly what to say and do without fear or hesitation. For this brief period of time you're super human.

The best place to witness momentum is watching a basketball game. I recall watching a game one night and half way through the fourth quarter I switched the channel because the score was a lopsided 85-70. The trailing team had been behind all night, and with time running out, it was obvious they were going to lose. An hour later I checked the NBA scores and to my astonishment, the trailing team had won the game 105-103.

What happened?

Simple…the force of momentum arrived in full force. And once the momentum shifts in your favor, your opponent is in trouble, and they know it. Some coaches will even call a time out just to try to shut it down…usually to no avail as momentum is an unstoppable force of nature.

So, your call list contains the seeds of momentum, and sets you up to make twenty to twenty-five calls an hour. That's a pretty good clip.

It's your compass in the job wilderness.

If you don't get through to someone, or the line is disconnected, or you get screened out by a gate keeper, keep driving forward by just dialing the next number. Do the math to figure out how many calls you can make in a week or a month. It's impossible to make this many calls without eventually getting a hit. Simply put, you are creating your own luck.

The fastest way to figure out who to call: ReferenceUSA

The easiest way to find the names of companies and their phone numbers is by visiting your local library. Ask the librarian if they provide any on-line resources for job seekers that provide names and addresses of companies. Explain to the librarian that you are looking for the names, addresses, and phone numbers of all the companies in a particular geographic area.

I did this at my local library and the librarian was super helpful. She showed me an excellent database (Reference USA) that I could even access from home with my library card—*for free*. To purchase this resource on my own would cost at least $500-$1500.

Here is a summary on how to put ReferenceUSA to work for you:

- Go to your local public library and get a library card. Use it to get on your local library website to access ReferenceUSA and any other company directories.
- ReferenceUSA not only contains the names of companies, but also key managers who work there and their phone numbers.
- Some libraries may carry online directories equal in quality to ReferenceUSA like Harris Selectory or Thomas Register. They may also carry good print directories, but many of these may be outdated.
- Compile a call list of twenty-five to thirty companies and simply call them using the script below.
- Spend most of your job hunting time calling hiring managers, not Human Resources.
- The more time you spend *talking* to a hiring manager instead of *emailing*, the greater your chances of getting a job offer.

Also, most communities have a free online Chamber of Commerce listing with a link out to company websites. To access your local Chamber, go out on Google and just type in the name of your city and the words, Chamber of Commerce. However, most Chamber directories don't have the depth of information like ReferenceUSA, Harris Selectory, or Thomas Register.

This cold calling script works like crazy to get through gate keepers

I created a simple cold-calling script that influences gatekeepers to put me right through to the hiring manager 90 percent of the time. In many cases, I don't even know the name of the manager.

I use a technique called pattern interrupt.

The best way to explain pattern interrupt is by understanding the psychology of approaching a receptionist or gatekeeper at the other end of the line. If you were a receptionist answering the phone all day long, you would quickly discover that everyone pretty much says the same thing when they call in.

Let's listen to a typical caller:

Receptionist: Good morning, XYZ Corp. How may I direct your call?

Caller: Yes, good morning...umm...would you please connect me to the engineering manager.

Receptionist: Who's calling?

Caller: Barbie Q

Receptionist: What company are you with?

Caller: Well, I'm not really with any company, this is a personal call. (Receptionist steps on the last three words of your sentence)

Receptionist: What's this in reference to?

Caller: I'm a mechanical engineer looking for a job and I thought I would…

Receptionist: Oh! You need to speak to Human Resources. Hold please! [click]

HR Admin: Hi, you've reached the voice mail of Claude Heinee in Human Resources. I'm either on the phone or away from desk. Please leave a message…

Caller: [Either hangs up or leaves a rambling voice mail message that never gets returned. After five or six of these calls, the caller gives up and washes the car.]

Here is what is going on in the mind of the gatekeeper. After hundreds of these kind of calls (not all job related), the receptionist's mind goes into auto-respond mode. The subconscious mind takes over and out pop the words, kind of like a robot. This is why most receptionists sound mechanical are not warm and chatty.

Toll booth collectors on the highways and byways respond to you the same way. Some don't even tell you to have a nice day anymore. (When are we going to stop saying that?)

When you use the pattern interrupt technique it throws the receptionist off. It's almost as if they are snapped out of a trance and actually have to think about how to handle this out-of-the-ordinary caller. All of a sudden you come across as someone extraordinary.

Let's listen in:

Receptionist: Good morning, XYZ Corp. How may I direct your call?

Caller: My name is Mike Petras (spoken calmly but authoritatively and with a tone of urgency). I'd like to speak with your engineering manager. Would you please direct me? (These three short sentences are spoken almost as one sentence with no pausing or hesitation.)

Comments: Here is what's going on in the mind of the receptionist in a split second. Who is Mike Petras? He sounds important. Maybe he's one of the executives of my company or a major customer. I *should* know this person. I don't want to challenge him/her if they are a VIP. I don't want to look foolish. The receptionist's next question (who's calling?) has already been answered, so their asking pattern has been altered. They are a little confused as to what to say.

Notice how I also tell the receptionist what to do by *directing* him/her to connect me to the engineering manager. So, now the receptionist feels a loss of control and is on the defensive, all in about three seconds. Amazingly, eight out of ten times they won't ask me another question. They will simply say, one moment please and put me through. Honestly!

The split second they tell me they are putting me through, I ask, *what is your engineering manager's name?* Again, they usually give it to me along with their extension or direct phone line. I've even had a few receptionists give me the manager's cell phone number!

Most receptionists are at the bottom of the corporate hierarchy and are used to taking orders from all kinds of people. The nature of their job is to help and facilitate. There is also a fair amount of turnover among receptionists. It's a thankless job as people can be pretty rude and condescending. So, most receptionists just want to make you happy and get on with the next call. Getting their cooperation is all in how you initiate the conversation.

You might be asking: But what if the receptionist does try to screen me? What should I say?

OK...fair question. About 75 percent of the time you will get another screening question.

Here is another example of the pattern interrupt technique with some push back:

Receptionist: Good morning, XYZ Corp. How may I direct your call?

Caller: My name is Mike Petras (spoken calmly but authoritatively and with a tone of urgency). I'd like to speak with your engineering manager. Would you please connect me? (These three short sentences are spoken almost as one sentence with no pausing or hesitation.)

Receptionist: What company are you with?

Caller: This is a personal call.

Receptionist: Can I tell him/her what this is about?

Caller: Sure, I'm a mechanical engineer (whatever your title or generic professional position) formerly with XYZ Corp and I'd like to speak with your manager about an engineering related issue. (Agreeing with them right off the bat disarms them and builds trust. They often will just put you right through.)

Comments: About half the time when you say: *"this is a personal call,"* the receptionist will go ahead and put you through. The other half of the time, they will press you further by asking you what your call is about. At this point, pattern interrupt works for you again because most people will get flustered and either lie, hem and haw, or simply collapse and confess they're a job seeker. As soon as this happens, the receptionist will just cast you into the HR black hole.

However, if you *immediately* agree to tell them what this is about in such a confident tone of voice, it has a disarming affect. By telling them you are a butcher, baker, or candlestick maker you solve their biggest fear... you're a salesman!

Heaven forbid the receptionist should put through a salesman to annoy their boss. So, most of the pressure is off and by simply telling them—in a most general kind of way—what it is you want to talk to the manager about, they feel comfortable putting you through.

Again, you've done nothing unethical or dishonest in any way. Every word of the above script is true. In fact, you are communicating very effectively.

One other thing before I share with you a good script to introduce yourself to the hiring manager. Let's assume you use the above script, but the receptionist is *really* tough today and asks another qualifying question.

Receptionist: Are you a customer or a supplier?

Caller: No, I'm not. This is a personal call (Don't be chatty...just answer the question).

Receptionist: Can you be more specific as to what this is about?

Caller: I really don't know how to explain it and would appreciate it if you would put me through.

Comments: If you use my pattern interrupt script, this type of dogged questioning only happens once every ten calls or so. You will encounter a couple of tough gatekeepers every once in awhile. If this happens and you don't know what to do, just collapse and tell them you're looking for some career advice from the manager. If they won't put you through or they dump you into Human Resources, just thank them, hang up, and move onto the next call on your list. Remember, nothing works 100 percent of the time. Also, don't get flustered and upset with the receptionist. They're just doing what they've been trained to do. If you actually knew this person, you would probably be good friends. Avoid reading too much into things.

Nine times out of ten the receptionist is going to put you through to the hiring manager. Only one problem: Half the time you're going to get voicemail.

Now what do you do?

There are two approaches you can take, leave a voicemail message or call back later to try and catch them at their desk. In a way this is a good problem because if you weren't successful in getting the manager's name, their voicemail greeting usually identifies them. Now you know their name which makes it ten times easier to get through the receptionist next time you call. It also makes it a cinch to navigate through an automated answering system.

I always leave a voicemail message because I want technology to work for me, and I have nothing to lose by leaving a message and everything to gain. If someone doesn't return my call, I can always call them back. But if I don't leave a message and they do have something, they'll never know I exist. The next time I call I might get another voicemail and time is marching on.

Most managers rarely sit behind their desks all day. They're in meetings, traveling, or out on the shop floor. So, I recommend you construct a voicemail script something like this:

"Hello Jane (use their first name so you come across as an equal instead of an underling), *you and I have never spoken before. I'm a mechanical engineer who lives locally and I'm looking for a position. I've researched XYZ Corp and I'm impressed with your products and reputation. I am a self-starter, I have my PMP certification, and I can solve complex problems quickly.* (This should come right out of your thirty second commercial we discussed in Chapter 4…I am…I have…I can]. *I would like to meet you to share with you how I can*

contribute to your growing success. You can reach me on my cell at…" (Always leave your cell number so you don't miss their call if they call you back. You may only get one shot at this.)

You should expect a ten to twenty percent call back rate with this message. Unlike HR, most hiring managers are good at returning calls. Often times you'll get a call back even if they don't have an opening. When this happens, go back to the networking script in Chapter 8 so you ask the right questions to get a referral or a key piece of information. Always try and get something of value out of every call to move you forward.

What do you say if the hiring manager answers the phone?

Use the same script as above. Make sure you've practiced it over and over out loud so it sounds natural and not too scripted. If the manager has an opening or is thinking about creating one, they will ask you to email to them your resume. When you're writing down their email address, ask them for the direct phone number so you can bypass the switchboard the next time you call.

Special Tip: Another reason to get a manager's direct dial is because two years from now you could be back on the job market. Using JibberJobber you still have all your notes, contacts, emails, phone numbers, and so on. Even if this manager has moved on, the new manager will likely be at this number. It saves you a lot of time and stress the next time you're job hunting. Also, you have this information at your fingertips to share with others if they call you to network. Lastly, if you click with the manager and have a good conversation, invite them to connect with you on LinkedIn.

Some job seekers do not like leaving voicemail and prefer to make their initial contact with the manager in a live setting. If you prefer this contact method, simply call every company on your list one right after the other until you finally connect with a real live person. After you've gone through your entire call list, start over again or wait a couple of hours and try again. Keep in mind that about 50 percent of the time your call will roll to voicemail. I know a few managers who never answer their phone during the day. Their boss or other key people know to call them on their cell phone.

Certain times of the day are better to call managers than others. For best results, try calling early in the morning (before most meetings commence), over the lunch hour (by-pass the switchboard), or late in the day (after 3:30, as they will be out of their meetings and following up on calls and emails at their desk).

Special Tip: If you prefer to talk with a real person, go through your call list three times. On the fourth try, if you get voicemail, leave a message. You have nothing to lose and everything to gain.

One last question before we move on. What if a manager's voicemail gives you their cell phone number...should you call it?

Why not? If they provided their cell number on their voicemail greeting, they are essentially telling you they prefer to be contacted on their cell. This may be the only way you'll ever connect with this manager. Do it!

When in doubt about whether or not to call someone, always ask yourself this question: What's the worst thing that could happen? In other words, create a horror scene in your mind.

In this case, you call the manager on their cell. They answer the phone and scream at the top of their lungs, *"You stupid idiot! How dare you call me on my private cell! What's your name and address?! I'm going to drive over to your house right now and punch you in the nose!"*

This is very extreme and downright ridiculous. We both know this isn't going to happen. Why would they have provided their cell to the public if it was so private and personal? Anyway, if this were to happen, how would you react?

Actually if someone reacted this way, they really would be doing you a favor. I sure wouldn't want to work for this person and would be grateful to find this out now rather than after I'm working there. But the best way to handle this would be to apologize for bothering them, hang up, and just make the next phone call on your list.

I've learned over the years that people who offend others are the ones with a problem...not me. So, I try not to take rude behavior too personal. My point in sharing with you this ridiculous scenario is sometimes we can become paralyzed by our fears...especially after our self-esteem is shot after being unemployed for eighteen months and hearing the word, NO, most of the time.

Having a good call list and a couple of calling scripts are like training wheels. They help you walk through your fears. Once you have a few private victories under your belt, your confidence comes back and it's easier to try new things and approach complete strangers.

Chapter 10:
You're Getting Job Interviews...Now What?

The purpose of our lives is to give birth
to the best which is within us.
~Marianne Williamson

When we started this journey together I compared myself to a batting coach and pledged my best efforts to help you get unstuck. Just as every great baseball player will experience a batting slump at least once in their career, job seekers will sometimes strike out too often just when they need a hit the most.

Hopefully, by now, you are hitting some singles and doubles.

Let's review the key points of the fastest way to find a job...and then...I want to talk with you about the next critical phase of your journey—hitting a home run in your job interviews.

1. You are *not* your job. Your whole life shouldn't be defined by what you do for a living. You will work again. This trial will make you a more complete, caring person.

2. Writing down your job loss story brings you closure and sets you up to move on. There is therapeutic value in writing down your feelings when you don't know what to do.

3. Create a warm and inviting work space to spark motivation and drive.

4. Your system of organization must be simple so nothing slips through the cracks, but also shouldn't be too detailed and burdensome.

JibberJobber is one of the best online tools to help you stay organized and manage your career after you find a job.

5. Embracing the ten habits of highly successful job seekers will keep you balanced, optimistic, and productive. Feelings of rejection and discouragement will be brief and easier to overcome.

6. Make a lasting first impression in thirty seconds. You can form a mind, but you can't change a mind. Poor communication skills are the number one reason why most candidates are rejected. You don't have to light up a room to win an offer, but you must be prepared to share your strengths and accomplishments clearly and concisely. You can learn this skill.

7. Less is more when it comes to creating a powerful resume. Content is king, but a good *look and feel* will make you stand out from other candidates.

8. You now know which job search methods work well and which ones fall short. You'll be able to rise above the noise, hype, and bad advice about job hunting. As a result, your attitude is positive and you're better equipped to handle rejection and indifference.

9. Social networking is not a buzz word or a time waster. It's the new way companies and recruiters look for candidates. It's important for you to participate in this cutting-edge employment trend. There is a learning curve to SN, but it is well worth your time and effort. The top three SN sites for job seekers are: LinkedIn, Facebook, and Twitter.

10. It's not *what* you know, but *whom* you know. You now have the tools to build a huge network of contacts who will be happy to help you. But you have to initiate the contact and consistently follow up. You can do this with confidence without annoying people.

11. Total strangers are approachable and will be glad to help you. You know how to find the movers and shakers in your industry and ask them for information, referrals, or advice.

12. Getting past gatekeepers is easy using the pattern interrupt method. It's an honest, ethical, straightforward way to get gatekeepers to put you through to hiring authorities. Most hiring managers are sweethearts who will listen to you…and occasionally interview and hire you. My calling script will give you the courage to call them.

13. When you're working again, help others and give back. Spend time with people on the phone if they call you in the middle of your workday. We're all too rushed these days. People who are hurting appreciate it if someone just listens and is kind.

True story: When I was going through my unemployment trial, I remember a day where I was really feeling down and discouraged. Out of the blue, a friend called me. He told me he had been thinking about me and had contacted a couple of friends to see if they could help me. He gave me their names and phone numbers and encouraged me to mention his name when I contacted them. Nothing came from these referrals, but this one call from my friend lifted my spirits and gave me renewed hope. To this day I'm grateful for his call. Simply reaching out to someone and having a conversation has the power to work a miracle in someone's life.

A new day has dawned for you. Your new job search approach is working. You're getting more interviews. This is encouraging after such a long drought. But if you bomb in your job interview, you'll never get an offer no matter how many interviews you score.

In other words, you've been tapped to sing in front of the judges on American Idol, but you had better dazzle them during your audition if you expect to be invited to Hollywood.

No worries. I have that job interview base covered for you, too.

I've created a comprehensive free website (http://www.job-interview-wisdom.com) to help you stand out from other candidates in your job interviews. My site also contains a daily blog and a free monthly newsletter.

My site is much more than job interview tips. It's a soft place to land for struggling job seekers and contains many true stories and examples.

I've listed over thirty of the top interview questions with detailed commentary on why each question is asked and how you should respond to impress your interviewer.

The best place to start on my site is the Site Map nav button located at the top of the left-hand vertical navigation bar. Every web page topic is listed and all of my newsletter (Job Brick Wall) back issues are listed. Now that my book is done, I'm going to be adding more content to my site and writing my next book.

It's been a pleasure working with you. I truly enjoyed writing this book and hope you prosper beyond your wildest dreams. There is nothing more gratifying to an author than knowing he made a difference in the lives of others. I am indebted to so many people for helping me over the years.

I would appreciate your honest feedback about my book and especially your success stories using these concepts. The best way to reach me is on my Contact Me page on my website.

All the best to you in your future endeavors. Blue skies and calm seas are on the horizon.

About the Author

Mike Petras is an author, professional career advisor, and executive recruiter. His popular website, www.job-interview-wisdom.com, provides job seekers with cutting-edge interviewing tactics to win job offers. Prior to recruiting and career coaching, Mike spent twenty years in the recreational vehicle industry as a regional sales director and national sales manager for Fleetwood Enterprises and Damon Corporation.

Mike hired, trained, promoted, and mentored over fifty sales professionals and staff support. Many of these individuals have since gone on to become directors, executives, and presidents of companies both inside and outside the RV industry.

For the past ten years Mike has also served as a volunteer employment specialist. He has conducted numerous community workshops for hundreds of job seekers and career changers resulting in breakthroughs when their job search had reached a dead end.

Mike majored in Economics at Indiana University. He currently resides in South Bend, Indiana, with his wife, Beth.